SINCERELY,
YOUR
AUTISTIC
CHILD

SINCERELY, YOUR AUTISTIC CHILD

*What People on the Autism Spectrum
Wish Their Parents Knew About
Growing Up, Acceptance, and Identity*

EDITED BY Emily Paige Ballou,
Sharon daVanport,
AND Morénike Giwa Onaiwu

Autistic Women
& Nonbinary Network

Beacon Press, Boston

BEACON PRESS
Boston, Massachusetts
www.beacon.org

Beacon Press books
are published under the auspices of
the Unitarian Universalist Association of Congregations.

26 25 24 23   12 11 10

This book is printed on acid-free paper that
meets the uncoated paper ANSI/NISO specifications
for permanence as revised in 1992.

Text design by Michael Starkman for
Wilsted & Taylor Publishing Services

Library of Congress Cataloging-in-Publication Data

Names: Ballou, Emily Paige, editor. | daVanport, Sharon,
    editor. | Onaiwu, Morénike Giwa, editor.
Title: Sincerely, your autistic child : what people on the autism spectrum
    wish their parents knew about growing up, acceptance, and identity /
    edited by Emily Paige Ballou, Sharon daVanport, and Morénike Giwa Onaiwu.
Description: Boston, Massachusetts : Beacon Press, 2021. | "Autistic Women
    & Nonbinary Network"—Title page. | Includes bibliographical references.
Identifiers: LCCN 2020049241 (print) | LCCN 2020049242 (ebook) | ISBN
    9780807025680 (trade paperback) | ISBN 9780807025697 (ebook)
Subjects: LCSH: Autistic children. | Parents of autistic children. |
    Friendship in children. | Autism spectrum disorders.
Classification: LCC HQ773.8 .S59 2021 (print) | LCC HQ773.8 (ebook) | DDC
    305.9/084—dc23
LC record available at https://lccn.loc.gov/2020049241
LC ebook record available at https://lccn.loc.gov/2020049242

This book is dedicated to
the autistic community of
our past, present, and future.
Those we've known and
those we haven't; those who
have gone without recognition,
support, or acceptance;
those who are using their lives
to be the change we all need;
and for those to come who
will build a better future.

It is also dedicated to one of
the authors, Mel Baggs, who
died before this was published.
Mel will be missed for hir
openness, humor, and creativity
as much if not more than
for hir tireless advocacy for
the disability community.

CONTENTS

FOREWORD

When parents come to me terrified, convinced there is no viable future for their precious children, I send them to those who not only wait to welcome our children with open arms, but who so willingly guide us as we make our way along this winding, rocky, beautiful path together.

A couple of years ago, I was asked to speak to a group of early education students at a local college. They were studying specialized teaching methodologies for Autistic students and, after bringing in an Autistic speaker, their professor wanted them to hear from a parent.

After I spoke, I opened the floor to questions. There was one I will never forget.

"How did you feel," a student asked, "when your daughter was first diagnosed with autism?"

I took a deep breath and answered honestly. "I was terrified," I said. "I sobbed. I retched over a toilet bowl. Because of everything that I thought that I knew about autism, I could not imagine that there was any real hope of a future for her."

I took another deep breath before I continued.

"Because, you see, I didn't know any better. I didn't yet know that the terrifying and damaging rhetoric out there about autism wasn't going to be our reality."

Desperate to find help for my newly diagnosed daughter, I turned to other parents, doctors, researchers, therapists—anyone who cared for or worked with Autistic individuals. While in some cases their experiences were helpful, the truth was that no matter how much or how hard they'd studied, how renowned their work or esteemed their opinions, they could still only offer the perspective I already had—that of a neurotypical person making assumptions about the Autistic experience from the outside in.

Some of the so-called experts sold outrageous myths as truisms, backed by the long-outdated idea that in order to exist, a human trait must be expressed only in a way that is familiar and recognizable to neurotypicals—to wit: intelligence measured only by language-rich tests, the existence of empathy determined only by its method of delivery, theory of mind "proven" by a test so flawed that it's not even wrong.

It soon became obvious that the current autism zeitgeist was off the mark. So I turned to the experts. The actual ones.

I searched for Autistic people who were able, in one way or another, to share their stories. As it turns out, they weren't hard to find. In fact, they were—and are—everywhere.

Some of the folks I found were verbal, some were non-speaking. Some used electronic devices to communicate, some were able, after having spent years, as my friend Barb Rentenbach likes to say, "disguised as poor thinkers" to type their thoughts.

I yearned to hear everything they had to say. More than anything, I longed to understand my daughter's experience not from the outside looking in but from the inside looking out.

It was on Brooke's fifth birthday that I published a post called "The Gift of Perspective."[1] It was only the second post that I ever wrote on my then-brand-new blog, A Diary of a Mom. In it, I quoted an Autistic woman who had anonymously published an article ahead of April, well known at the time as Autism Awareness Month. She wrote, "Don't pity me or try to cure or change me. If you could live in my head for just one day, you might weep at how much beauty I perceive in the world with my exquisite senses. I would not trade one small bit of that beauty, as overwhelming and powerful as it can be, for 'normalcy.'"[2]

"I always feel so privileged," I wrote in response, "to get glimpses into the minds and hearts of people who have lived through this. When someone says, 'I wouldn't change it for the world,' well, what an amazing reminder that every bit of this struggle (both real and perceived) is SUBJECT TO PERCEPTION."

My daughter was five when I wrote those words. She had little to no novel language. Her life was often frustrating and overwhelming and painful and hard. It was a life-changing moment.

Over the years, I have become increasingly grateful to those who give so generously of their time and precious energy to share some of the most intimate details of their lives in the name of a better world for their younger brethren. I don't know what I would have done without their insight, their guidance, and their friendship. I cannot imagine the parent I would be today without having had their help in stripping away my own assumptions, my own ableism, and my deeply ingrained neurotypical bias in order to understand and respect my child's inner life.

Their experiences may not be an exact match with hers. Some may not even come close. But always—always—there is invaluable insight to be gained from their writing: a glimpse of what it means to be Autistic in a predominantly neurotypical world.

There is no greater resource for neurotypical parents of Autistic children than the members of their own community. When parents come to me terrified, convinced there is no viable future for their precious children, this is where I send them: to those who not only wait to welcome our children with open arms, but who so willingly guide us as we make our way along this winding, rocky, beautiful path together.

They know, like no one else possibly can, of what they speak.

Jess Wilson

LETTER FROM THE EDITORS

When we first set out to publish *What Every Autistic Girl Wishes Her Parents Knew* under our imprint, DragonBee Press, it was during a time in which there seemed to be a hopeless division between autistic adults and non-autistic parents. The relationship between autistic adults and parents of autistic kids has in the past been marked by misunderstanding and lack of a common language and sense of possibility for the lives of autistic kids. Since many of us had grown up in a time period in which autistic and intellectually/developmentally disabled youth were often segregated in school, institutionalized, and undiagnosed, or our disabilities treated with shame and hidden sometimes even from us, many parents of newly diagnosed young people had either never known—or never known that they'd known—other autistic people or what our lives could look like from early childhood all the way to later adulthood. As such, they didn't understand how to relate their own autistic kids to autistic adults (including strangers on the internet) asking them to parent differently.

But as a community of autistic people who were diagnosed or identified both early and later in life ourselves, who have found community and solidarity in each other, in many ways members of our organization, AWN, are uniquely equipped to reach out and let parents know that many of the most important sources of strength and support for building a good life were almost never a particular kind of therapy or clinical intervention. Instead, we draw strength from knowing that we are accepted by the people in our lives, the recognition of our full humanity, and chances to be genuinely included in the world around us.

With increasing recognition over the years of the historic under-diagnosis of certain segments of the community (such as autistic women and girls) came an increase in awareness that autistic people themselves could actually have children; many parents of autistic kids were actually autistic, but undiagnosed. In fact, several of our own authors are not just autistic people but are parents (biological and adoptive) of autistic children themselves, and their vital knowledge is shaped not only by their own autistic childhoods but by their experiences as parents.

Another issue we knew we needed to address with the anthology re-publication is the increasing affirmation of gender diversity within the autistic community. When AWN was founded (as the Autism Women's Network), and when we first conceived of the original anthology, our organization was dedicated to addressing the disparities in recognition, diagnosis, and social support faced by autistic women and girls in a medical and professional culture that often presented the stereotype of a non-verbal, young, white boy as the face of what autism meant, actively erasing and obscuring the existence and experiences of autistic girls and adult women.

Current research suggests that people on the autism spectrum demonstrate a diverse range of gender expression and sexual orientation. It is also true that the people who have gone underserved and unrecognized in the mainstream discussion of autism aren't just cisgender women and girls. And even when we are raised as girls or identify as girls for some part of our lives, these are experiences that impact us growing up even if we don't yet have the language to explain our gender realities.

We still very much believe that our initial vision to serve autistic women and girls is an important and meaningful one. However, the last several years have proven that in order to fulfill and be true to our original purpose, we needed to become a more gender-inclusive organization. It is also the defining reason we changed the name of our organization from the Autism Women's Network to the Autistic Women & Nonbinary Network (AWN, or AWN Network), a name that is reflective of our renewed mission.

What our authors have to say is relevant for autistic kids of every gender, which is why our title *What Every Autistic Girl Wishes Her Parents Knew* is now *Sincerely, Your Autistic Child.* As you read the different chapters in this book, please keep in mind that each writer has offered to share a part of who they are as a person so that you may better understand what autistic people experience as we navigate the world. Because we believe it is important to highlight the impact of identity on our lives, our anthology intentionally features a diverse group of authors. With writers ranging from the Silent Generation to Generation Z, we strive to provide a multigenerational lens; similarly, we seek to represent a broad range of faith beliefs with contributors who are Muslim, atheist, Jewish, agnostic, Christian, Pagan, etc.

We have authors who are advocates, stay-at-home and working parents, college students, employed, and unemployed; we have authors who live independently, who have live-in support, who live with their partner, spouse, or family, and who live (or have lived) in residential or congregate care. Additionally, we are proud to feature a myriad of cultural backgrounds in our anthology. We have authors from the UK, Canada, and Japan in addition to the US; half are people of color (including Asian, Latinx, Black, Indigenous, Arab, and multiracial people) and half are white. Our authors include individuals who are non-speaking (both exclusively and part-time) and use adaptive and augmentative communication (AAC) technology such as typing, and individuals who communicate by speaking.

You will notice that some writers refer to themselves as "autistic"; others say "on the spectrum" and some use "has autism." Although AWN, as an organization, has adopted identity first language (i.e., "Autistic"), we believe that people have the right to choose how they identify. You'll also see some authors capitalize "Autistic" in a similar way that many Deaf or Black people capitalize those terms out of a sense of identity or pride. You may notice that some of our contributors use personal pronouns other than "she/her" or "he/him," including "they/them" or "sie/hir."

These are choices sometimes made by transgender, agender, and gender non-binary people when conventional binary language about gender does not reflect their personal reality. Finally, wherever functioning level language is used ("high-functioning" or "low-functioning"), it is to discuss language that clinicians and medical professionals have used, not because AWN endorses the ideas conveyed by those terms.

Our anthology is designed to offer the reader a break from the clinical/medical guidebooks to consider perspectives that are only available by hearing from the real experts, autistic people. As no two individuals or families are the same, each experience shared in this book is authentically unique.

Sincerely, Your Autistic Child is a dedicated labor of vulnerability, honesty, and love, and AWN is thrilled to reintroduce this book to you!

Early Memories, Childhood, and Education

1 Acknowledge Vulnerability; Presume Competence

B. Martin Allen

I have a place in this world. The fact that I am here is proof of that. Trust that we will find that place, together.

———

I WAS YOUNG ONCE, and all I knew was what others told me. I grew up not knowing that my needs were valid. I grew up in a world where I was defective and unable to justify my existence. As an adult, as a parent, I know no one needs to justify my children's existence. We exist, full stop, no qualifiers needed. What follows is clearly not an account of what a younger me would have wished adults knew, because I could not know. I offer instead what I *needed* adults to know, colored by the hindsight I've developed over the years as a parent—and now as a grandparent.

Expectation

I can feel your resentment. If I am not the child you wanted, if you feel your life has been made unfairly difficult, I feel that. Throw out all those damning words of diminished hope foisted upon you by people who call themselves experts. If you believe them, I will, too. If you love me, but you wish . . . that wish is a barrier, too. It serves as a roadblock to your love.

I may not be capable of toughening up. Exposing me to sensory onslaught only drains my reserves. I will not develop an immunity to sensory or emotional pain simply by prolonged exposure, even if that exposure is called therapy. I need safe spaces. I will be better equipped to take risks and test my limits if I know there is a real safety net under me.

3

I need to learn and grow at my own pace. I know you've heard this before, but uneven skill sets are a real thing. The linear timeline of what is learned when it is, is a guideline, not fact. Don't waste energy worrying over what I can't do, and don't let that hold me back from fully exploring what I can do.

Your fears may not be reality. Stay aware and protect me, but don't fall into the trap of thinking that I am so different that you are the only one who could possibly see me as special. If I am wonderful enough for you to love me, others will see that as well. Not everyone is making fun of me. Not everyone is a potential abuser. Do not protect me so much that I do not have room to connect with others. Even if I struggle with much-vaunted life skills at ten, or fifteen, or forty, do not let your imagination project that into some nightmare adulthood for me. I have a place in this world. The fact that I am here is proof of that. Trust that we will find that place, together.

Connection

If I only know people with no known disabilities, I cannot help but question my worth by sheer deductive reasoning. I need to know others like me, to know I am not alone. I need that connection, but do not be troubled or confined by a narrow definition of this. I may find other autistics whose autism looks different from mine. Even if it's hard for you to see how alike we are, we will see our shared experience. I might find other friends in the broader disabled community. We are more alike than different. Some of these people may be older than me, and I can learn from their wisdom. Some may be younger, and I will be their role model. I may make these friends in person or online. All interactions hold value. The point is, broaden the scope in your search for my community. Let me know that in a sea of sameness, I am one of the many, many different, and in that variation lies beauty.

Autonomy

In my relationship with you, I need to have the power to say no. Yes, you are still the parent, and I do not always know what is in my best interests. Having ownership of No is not the same as getting whatever I want, but rather an affirmation of that very human need for autonomy. Autonomy is dignity. Autonomy says I am a whole, valued person who is as worthy of a place on this planet as any other human. I need to freely practice this skill and see my No paired with your unconditional love. This will build strength and resilience that will carry me long after you are no longer there to hold my hand.

However, even if you respect my No, others will not. I exist in a world where sexism and ableism are used to prop up one another. My No will be discounted. Autism will be used as an excuse to validate this violation of my autonomy. When I say No, I will be told I am being mean, thoughtless, or selfish; that I do not understand. I will be told this by teachers, bosses, and potential suitors alike. You, too, navigate this emotional manipulation, often without having to give it much thought, but it will not be so clear to me. Show me. Teach me to recognize it. This will not leave me bitter and cynical if done in a loving and open way. It will provide me with the tools I need in adulthood.

Competence

Presuming competence is critical. It is a cornerstone of respect. That does not mean it is easy. Often, people who want to embody this ethic, people who truly believe they live this principle, will find at times that they fall short. The presumption of competence is not an act that can be completed. It is an exercise, a constant work in progress. To practice this principle, you will need to keep your heart open to being wrong. Your ego may need a gut check. I promise, it is worth it. I will grow in beautiful ways if this is the practice of those around me.

In a perfect world, we would all be guided by the presumption of competence, not just in regard to disability but in all human interaction. But we do not live in a perfect world. In the real world, no matter what skills I acquire—be they social, emotional, physical, or educational—there will be a sizable number of people who will presume me to be incompetent. Brace me for it. Make sure I know my rights. Let me know over and over again that I am so much more than the box some small-minded person wishes to fit me into. Practice with me the interactive tools I need to stand up in the face of those who do not believe in me.

2 It's Us Against the World, Kid

Brigid Rankowski

My mother has always been my biggest ally. She is always there for me, even when the world seems to be against me.

AS BEST AS I CAN REMEMBER, my parents ended up raising me in two different ways. My father tried to raise me to blend into the sea of normalcy. He said he wanted me to "fit in," but what he really wanted was for me to not stand out. That's a big difference. Standing out as someone different made him look different, and for that, he was ashamed. This shame made him angry at not having a "perfect" child, and the anger was sometimes directed at me. This shame complex stays with me even now as I stress out about looking "weird" at times. It's been ingrained in the deep corners of my thoughts, to strive for "normal."

My mother is an artist and raised me to believe I could be anything in the whole world. She taught me every color was special because it was unique and nothing else was the same color. She showed me that everyone was the same and everyone was different in their own way. Different was not a bad thing; different was the amazing part of nature that created diversity. "Normal" was nothing to strive for, and it actually bored my mother. From a young age, she knew I was unlike my friends and thought I was amazing because of that fact. My relationship with her is more one of equals than of the parent–child bond I often see with my friends.

Growing up, it was not obvious I was on the autism spectrum. Labeled with learning disabilities from an early age, things were always more difficult for me compared to my peers. Every Tuesday morning, I would miss the beginning of classes in my private school to go to speech class at a local public school. To this day, I'm not sure what, if anything, my classmates were told of my absence. When I was young, doctors hooked me up to heart monitors because they thought I had a severe heart defect. I would be randomly debilitated with chest pain and difficulty breathing, and I was unable to function during these spells. Years later, my family and I learned this was just the extreme anxiety to which I am prone. Anxiety can still be so debilitating that it closely mimics an epileptic seizure.

People always remark on my social skills and wonder how I can be on the spectrum. I just laugh and remember the countless hours spent glued to my television mimicking the characters on the screen. My skills of echolalia and mimicry helped me "pass" for years until the fateful day when all my coping skills went away. My parents would take me to theater productions as often as possible when they found out how connected to the arts I truly was. My father would take me because he was able to boast about his cultured child who knew all the lines to every play after only one performance, while my mother saw how completely absorbed I became in every bit of action on stage.

Years later, my mother remains the rock of my family and she completely promotes my unconventional lifestyle. She's trying to make her living as an artist and is quite proud of me for finally acknowledging my artistic abilities. When I called my mother from the cornfields of Iowa, telling her I wanted to go back to performing after several years prioritizing my health, her response was, "It's about time."

I'm unable to work a "normal" job due to a car accident that caused my multiple disabilities to worsen, yet I do keep myself busy with various special interests. My many activities include being a fire show producer, helping run a nonprofit social circus, acting as a professional mermaid, advocating while on state and national boards, writing articles on a myriad of topics, and of course breathing fire or spinning fire. My mother is one of my biggest supporters when it comes to my many different artistic pursuits and will tell anyone she meets about her "Fire Breathing Mermaid" of a daughter.

There are days I crave normalcy and dream of a nine-to-five life where the most exciting thing planned for the week is pizza night on Friday. The thing I most often wish was "normal" has always been my social skills. The social quirks I have of speaking what's on my mind and being completely oblivious are not always so charming to me. They can lead to depression, as I sometimes feel isolated in a room full of people who all seem to be speaking in a foreign code. People speak in looks and "you knows" instead of using real words.

Seeking a good education, I spent my high school years at an all-girls private school. As a person who doesn't understand the complexities of normal social interactions, let alone the minefield of social interactions in an all-female population, this was a special type of torture. Suddenly thrown into the chaotic ocean of hormones and scholastic competition instead of male attention, I, at times, found myself drowning. Due to health reasons, stress, anxiety, and brain damage, I missed a total of 279 days of school during my time in high school. It should be noted I made honor roll almost every quarter, leading to one staff member's comment in an IEP (Individualized Education Program) meeting of, "Imagine how well she'd do if she actually came to school?" As amused as my mother and I were, the other staff members did not find this statement equally hilarious.

As you read this, you'll notice my mother is mentioned quite a lot. Before, I said our relationship was more peer-like instead of the classic parent–child relationship, and this requires greater emphasis to understand why I turned out the way I did. My father was not a healthy man, and this quickly turned to abuse. Blaming the faults—existent or nonexistent—of his family members shifted the responsibility for his actions away from himself. He became physically violent by the time I was in first grade, and this escalated until he was finally kicked out of the home shortly after my sixteenth birthday. The physical violence was random, but the emotional and verbal abuse was a daily occurrence. His biggest insult, the one that always hit home the hardest, was "Why won't you just be normal?"

I was seeing a therapist when we finally had enough of my father and were able to have him removed from the home. At one point, my therapist asked my mother to come into the room, as he had something he wanted to tell her. He had also noticed how often I spoke of my mother as a confidant and ally. I will always remember the words that came out of his mouth. He looked at us and said, "It seems like you two have an 'us against the world' mentality going on."

My mother and I looked at each other, nodding our heads in agreement. This man thought it was a negative thing, but this is the greatest gift my mother has ever given me. She is my rock and has always stepped up to support me, even when the odds were against me or when my version of events varied so significantly from other people's stories. There were times in my life, and there still are moments, when I need my mother to translate what is going on in my head into a version the general population can understand. There are also times when the actions of those around me confuse me so much that I need someone to help me understand the world around me. My mother does this for me.

People often come up to me after I give a presentation in which I mention my mother, and they compliment my mother to the ends of the earth. My mother refuses to take any credit for the person I have become, because she says she only gave me the tools to be great. Why would you take credit for someone building a birdhouse when all you did was give them the materials to do so? Well, because my mother gave me the right tools, and she still does. She always encouraged me to stand up and say something when I saw something wrong. From a young age this led me to stand up to bullies and work with animal shelters. She taught me it was always best to be honest, but that there is a time and place to be honest, especially about delicate matters. One of my favorite things, which she still shows me, is how being nice to people and acting polite will always work better than getting angry with people who are being rude. All of these things are ways my mother has modeled strong characteristics to me. Kids on the spectrum really pick up on role models, so it's important to have a wide variety of positive ones. Some of my mother's friends were friends of mine because I enjoyed talking about art instead of the latest cartoon.

One of the biggest challenges of being on the spectrum may have to do with the lack of theory of mind. We can't understand what's in peoples' heads. This can mean that when we do great things, we often don't recognize our own hard work. We really need someone to tell us when we do good things, even the little things. Praise is a good thing and promotes self-esteem as well as confidence. These are very important traits that everyone should have; they are like the armor we need to deal with the world around us.

Some days it's difficult and we get frustrated by our differences. Everyone has bad days. At times we wish things were easier for us, and this can make us depressed and generally sad. Embracing positivity and the strengths of being Autistic is important because that is who we are. Being Autistic is something that will never change. The right thing for a parent to do is to help their child celebrate who she is and help them love themselves.

The greatest thing that a parent can do is support their child. Let your child know how amazing they are and how much you believe in them. It really does seem so simple, but it makes a world of difference. I've met hundreds of people on the spectrum and hundreds more who are not. Most everyone I've met says they wish their parents were more supportive and loved them unconditionally. Most parents do love their children, but it is important to let them know verbally, because we don't always pick up on nonverbal cues. Yes, as difficult as it is to say it, we sometimes do not know when people care about us or love us.

Many of my friends have met my mother, and now she's friends with many of them. She lets people know that if they need parental support, she is there for them in ways their own parents may not be. My mother has always been my biggest ally. She is always there for me, even when the world seems to be against me. So no matter what happens in my life or how badly I mess up or who breaks my heart or how scared I am, my mother will always be there with her shoulder to cry on and a hug. In moments that really do come down to us against the world, I'm very comfortable with my odds.

3 What Autistic Girls Wish Their Parents Knew About Friendship

Jane Strauss

I knew that it was not necessary or even usual for one to have large numbers of friends.

▬▬▬▬▬

ONE OF THE THINGS that many parents seem to be unhappy about when their child is labeled "Autistic" is this: "But they will not have play dates." Friendship, "socializing," and human interaction are seen as central to our very humanity. Females often fly under the radar for being labeled on the autism spectrum because their social development is different from that of males, generally resulting in more social orientation, better imitation skills at a younger age, and earlier speech, of whatever kind, than their male counterparts.

In modern society—where doing things in groups seems to have become the norm—parent education, daycare, and early childhood programs result in children being put into groups at ever-younger ages. The groupification of society results in challenges for any person who has sensory issues or does not like change. And those in charge of such programs, in my experience, are not very good at dealing with such folk, no matter how young. I still remember the extreme confusion of staff at our local "Early Childhood Family Education" program where my eldest daughter spent the entire time I was in the parent group screaming instead of interacting and exploring. The only time she did not scream was if the room she was in had a fan or a similar rotating object, which I suspect she used as a stim.

This being the case, and as in most modern societies where females are held to a higher standard of social behavior than males, girls on the spectrum are even more likely to be pushed socially than boys—if they are even identified. In addition, the huge amount of energy it takes to behave in a "social butterfly" manner is often ignored or overlooked. Especially if it has not been difficult for Mom to make friends, easily interact, or read social cues, her daughters seem ever more alien when they do not adopt those behaviors easily or naturally. Sometimes Mom has had challenges making friends but has nonetheless muddled through. She may or may not see herself in her daughter. And often those on the spectrum become chronic targets for bullies, even when they have not been labeled, or are not considered disabled enough for their quirks to "count."

It is no accident that Autistic girls are more often labeled with depression or eating disorders than with their real neurodivergent natures. When, from early childhood, you live out of sync with social norms and expectations, it's easy to feel as if you are alien, wrong, and bad. In such a situation, one would have to be catatonic *not* to be at least a little depressed.

As an Autistic woman who struggled through over five decades before being properly identified, and who learned, through trial and error, about friends, friendship, what they are, and what they are *not*, there are a number of things I wish that my parents had known and had been able to teach me. These include how to make friends, how to tell if people really are friends, how to deal with bullies and bullying (as I have learned that often institutions don't do this effectively), and that it is okay not to live in herds. The one thing my parents tried to teach and seem to have done a reasonably good job of is Shakespeare's old statement: "This above all, to thine own self be true."

What would I suggest that parents know or do? Here you go . . . and there is no "whole body listening" or "theory of mind" involved in any of them.

First, you might wish to take a long, hard look at yourself if your support systems seem inadequate and you are struggling. Autism does run in families, so far as we know. Until recently, many females skated under the radar, and you just might be one of them.

Getting support for yourself can be and is, in the long run, better for your children, whichever gender they may be. And as you learn to cope, you will be a better role model for your child.

Second, realize that your daughter is an individual with her own strengths and weaknesses, and that she is not a smaller version of you. No, really. She may well be introverted and dislike being in large groups. The stress of dealing with noise, motion, and even flickering lights can result in an inability to cope at all and obvious withdrawal. Or, she may seem to do well, until she is at home, where she explodes. Remember, stress can cause a delayed response, bursting out once she is in a safe place.

If large groups seem to result in stress, put those off and preferentially deal with small groups. Yes, Virginia, you can have play dates for your child, they just may be more low-key than you thought they "should" be. An hour or less interacting with a single child while the moms have coffee is perfectly fine as a play date.

A piece of old research I wish parents knew about is that kids on the spectrum are often more comfortable with playmates chronologically younger than themselves. That does make sense, if you look at the spectrum as a developmental delay relative to the mythic norms. Delay does not mean never developing; it does mean doing so more slowly than usual. This may change the nature of play dates, but your child's time playing with a child two or three years younger than herself is still interaction, and may be more beneficial to both than pushing them to interact in a group of age mates.

All of my own children showed at least traits of if not full-blown autism, four of them in the years when sensory issues were emerging as a thing and before the *Diagnostic and Statistical Manual of Mental Disorders* (DSM) categories for autism (apart from cognitive impairment) even existed. Our family's first response to this was to avoid large, group childcare when childcare was needed. We joked that we had managed to find the smallest existing licensed daycare in the entire city that did not include a nanny at home. In a group of four to five, our kids thrived. Once they reached preschool age, again, small groups of fewer than ten were the norm for us. All were in the mainstream, with the exception of the one who narrowly qualified for early intervention after being found "too hyper" to be acceptable for a Waldorf preschool in which her older sister fit in well.

I strongly recommend that in the early years, children not be separated out from the broad range of others, and that their deficits not be emphasized, although limiting group size is usually helpful. The best goal of early intervention, properly executed, is to identify barriers to growth and find ways of getting around them. It is not to separate children with challenges or differences from others. It is not to emphasize the negative characteristics, and it is not to make those children the "other." Doing so, in my experience, results in bullying, depression, isolation, and lifelong stress.

Third, I wish parents knew about the option to teach their children at home or at least to look for small learning environments in which their children's challenges will not be held against them. My daughters were all delayed in their motor skills. The one who completed kindergarten was treated as though she were "not quite bright" because she performed poorly at all the gross and fine motor skills tests that the schools thought were mandatory to pass at five years of age. Expectations for her were low, and I had to constantly fight the schools and their assumptions, despite her *lacking* a label. Her ability to learn improved immensely once I brought her home for learning, and the other children were not put in school until they had completed at least several years at home. As a home educating family, we were able to have somewhat more control over who the children spent time with and under what circumstances and arrange for them to meet a wide variety of people of different ages. We went on field trips, met with other homeschoolers, and did volunteer work; 4H, religious school, summer camp programs, community education, park programs, and art classes rounded out learning opportunities.

Our family then put all the children in a very small non-public (as it happened, religious) school in which no class was larger than twelve students. They thrived there, and from that base continued on in carefully selected public options for secondary school, with three of them placed in a small learning environment of the "open" type, where creativity and individual quirks were valued, and one in a highly structured academic program. All developed friendships in those schools, through meeting others with like interests, and they all learned to advocate for themselves when they did encounter bullies. All have since continued in post-secondary education, pursuing their respective passions.

Similarly to my own children, I had the possible advantage of having been labeled in middle adulthood, and having not spent my early years in special education, where the authorities often keep students separated and, based on what some of my friends have said, teach dysfunctional "social skills." This may be why I knew that it was not necessary or even usual for one to have a large number of friends. It seemed normal to me to have one or two close friends and some acquaintances, rather than traveling in a mob. I am still in touch, fifty years later, with a friend from grade school, and I have friends from high school, college, and a variety of other points in my life. I have successfully raised four kids on the spectrum to adulthood and they have found their places in the world. Unlike many in the world, I have been divorced only once and have maintained long-term romantic relationships as well. That said, I have come up with several skills and behaviors that I recommend, based upon my decades of experience, which I have shared with younger spectrumites, and I respectfully suggest that parents would do well to know and share these six guidelines.

1. **Take part in activities you like, if possible, outside of your room.** If you like gaming, do that. If social fear means you have to start online, by all means do, but look for gaming groups, conventions, clubs, and meet-ups, so that you can meet people in the real world. Take small steps, as it profits nothing if panic at dealing with the world means you are not enjoying yourself.

In high school, my friends were also involved in orchestra, theater, art, Scouts, and folk music groups. We started out with interests we had in common and we were able to build interactions and relationships on our commonalities. In college, I made friends with people in the Outing Club, as I liked climbing, hiking, and camping. It's best to try to get involved with a group that meets on a regular basis—weekly, monthly, etc.—or more often, as with performing groups. As an adult, I have met people through science fiction and community interests.

2. **Do not take part in something you do not like to do, *just* to meet people.** One example is going to bars. If you don't like drinking alcohol or being around people who do, then don't go to bars to meet people there. Another is going to large parties if you don't like noise or crowds. I have found that doing those kinds of things leaves me unhappy and sets me up for failure.

Think of it this way:

- If you like doing the activity, then you
  will be more likely to enjoy going to do it.

- When you enjoy the activity, you will be more likely
  to look happy, and people are more likely to approach
  and want to meet people who are smiling.

- Sometimes you might even forget your anxiety
  in meeting people who share your interests.

I met both my partners through science fiction activities that I enjoyed. There are many unique personalities in these groups, and we raised the children attending the activities within this community, which provided learning and association opportunities that were not otherwise available. One advantage these days is that science fiction and fantasy have become mainstream in my lifetime, so they are now considered just another interest and do not separate fans as far from society as was the case in the 1950s, '60s, and even '70s.

3. **If you do not understand something a potential friend does or says, ask them what they mean.** There is nothing so sad as losing a potential friend through a misunderstanding. This is the case whether you may have misunderstood something they said or if they may have misstated it. Remind your daughter that she may take something literally that is not meant to be taken in that way, so it is better to check on meanings than to be hurt without need. Similarly, if a statement truly is cruel or meant to be hurtful, it is best to know this and consider if the person who said it really is worth the time to develop a friendship with.

4. **Remember that getting to know someone does take time.** Even if it feels to you as if you must become best friends within a week or two, this is not realistic. Try to let the other person take the lead on getting together.

   This does not mean that if you will be going someplace fun that you think they might also like and want them to come along, you don't ask. It does mean that you might not succeed if you think you should get together every day or even every week when you have first met. They have other people in their life, and it looks like stalking if you try to monopolize their time. That can get you into trouble.

5. **Not everyone will be kind to you and learning to identify when they are not being kind is a useful survival skill.** Some people may be unsure of themselves and try to make themselves feel more important by putting others down. They may think it is funny to make another person think they are friends and then behave in a nasty or exclusionary way. Sometimes when you think people are excluding you, they really are. Role-playing or practicing ways to respond to bullying and nasty behavior can be useful. Teaching that bullying reflects more on the person doing it than on the person being bullied is useful, too. Starting early on with books such as *My Name Is Not Dummy*, by Elizabeth Crary, a "make your own decision" social story written in the 1980s, can be helpful.[1]

6. **Be nice to people.** You never know where friends may come from. Sometimes "popular" people may be imitating others or saying mean things about them behind their backs, saying that they are "just joking," and you think that joining in will make you popular, too. It won't. It will just make you as mean as they are. Try to find people who are kind to others, watch what they do, and copy them. In the long run they make the best friends, to you and to others, and are models for how you can be a good friend, too. And being nice to your friends is a good start to keeping them over the long term.

4 What Your Daughter Deserves: Love, Safety, and the Truth

Kassiane Asasumasu

She needs love from her parents, not yet another person she can't quite please.

PARENTS OF AUTISTIC GIRLS, obviously you want to do right by your daughter, or you'd not be reading this. Here are things my parents would have needed to know to make my life easier. *They* didn't know, but you do. This is my gift to you and to your child.

Most overarchingly, know that our self-esteem is fragile. No one likes being exasperating, and we know we are perceived that way. Most children want to please adults and want other children to like, or at least not hate, them. Autistic children are still children, and this pattern holds for us. We were plopped into a world where everyone and everything tells us we're wrong for completely incomprehensible reasons. This gets exhausting very quickly and it breaks us down faster than you can imagine.

The evil twin to our fragile self-esteem? We learn very early on that what we are isn't what you wanted when you became a parent. You can readjust your dreams, hopes, and expectations, and you can love us fiercely, but we know we're not what you really desired. Please don't tell your child that she's all you ever dreamed of in one moment and send her to hours of coercive, damaging therapy meant to change who she is in the next. These do not add up. We *know* these don't add up.

To take these things into account, you need to pick and choose any therapies with the utmost care. So many therapy options seek to change us into the child you *did* want at any cost. They won't succeed at this. There is no therapy that can make us the effortlessly socially adept, smiley, precocious child that everyone dreams of. These are therapies that will drive home that this is our failure. They will make us anxious, acutely aware of our endless failure to meet expectations, and teach us that to be okay we need to do anything and everything we're told. This is a profoundly dangerous message.

Hold your daughter dear. Do not allow anyone to teach her that unquestioning compliance is what is expected of her. If you raise her to believe she has no right to say no, she will take you at your word. Not everyone is a predator, but predators can sense women whose boundary-setting skills were systematically demolished from ten miles away. Add to that a lack of self-esteem from a lifetime of being what was not wanted.

No, you want better for her. She's young now; adulthood seems so far away. But every day of childhood is practice for adulthood. We're vulnerable. We need extra boundary-setting practice. We need to learn this skill with people who would never hurt us, so when we need to stand up to those who would, we know how. And we need to know that we deserve to be safe. You're charged with teaching your daughter that. If she learns nothing else, make sure she learns that her body is her own, that she deserves to be safe, and that if someone hurts or scares her, they are the one at fault.

So many other things you need to know come right back to these two core concepts: Your daughter is an amazing human being and she has a right to boundaries and safety. You need to know that if she wants friends, she wants *friends*—equals. Many young autistic girls find themselves a "project" of their age peers. Please don't let this be her only social interaction. Don't act like the popular girl who wants to "fix" your daughter is the bee's knees. This dumps a lot of salt into the "not the child you hoped for" wound. That other girl is not your child, and *your* child is so much more than a project. Being "worked on" is demeaning. It is not equal. This is a terrifying boundary to draw when you know it will disappoint your parents and likely have negative social repercussions as well. Encourage peer relationships that are equal and mutually beneficial. Your girl doesn't need to be a mimic of her "queen bee" peers. She needs to be the best damn her she can be.

All girls—indeed all children—need role models. They need adults they can look up to and aspire to be like. Most little girls meet a number of women and older girls they can successfully emulate. Many autistic girls . . . don't. Your daughter needs to see adults like her. She may never be like her teachers, her auntie, her babysitter, her neighbors, or any of the women who she is around very much. The skills and interests demonstrated by and encouraged for girls are often incompatible with our disabilities.

Make friends with autistic women. Your little girl needs to see adults she can be like. She needs to know adults who are profoundly joyful at minutia, who have executive functioning difficulties, who stim, who don't play the social games in the standard way. She needs to know adults like her exist. She needs us as a guide. And she needs to know that her parents *like* the kind of person she will grow up to be. Thinking your family would avoid you if they weren't stuck with you? It aches. That "not the child my parents wanted" thing? It's easier to believe your mother when she tells you that you're exactly what she dreamed of when her friends get you and are on your wavelength.

And your daughter, she needs someone in her life who understands effortlessly. You can be exploding with love for her, and she can reciprocate, think you are the best parents on earth, but that doesn't mean you can do all she needs. And that is okay. Children need communities. Help her connect to other adults. It is an act of love to help her meet and bond with adults of her neurology. To know someone who has been there is a gift. To not feel alone is more precious than diamonds. We so often feel alone. The diagnosis rates of autism in girls still lag, and we're usually not particularly like Autistic boys. We're so often alone, but we don't have to be. Our people are out there. Help your girl find hers before she resigns herself to never being understood.

I'm sure you're trying to understand her, but there are things allistic[1] parents can't instinctively wrap their heads around. She needs you to try. Her needs are real. She's doing the best she can with what she has. She's trying at least as hard as a non-Autistic child.

She may have you convinced she understands things she doesn't. We're good at that, we Autistic girls. Our masking mechanisms are often successful enough to fool our parents. If your daughter is good at words, she may have you convinced that she understands school or people, things that she doesn't. If she's like me in this regard, she may even *think* she has a clear understanding of things that she doesn't have: fiction, how to write a term paper, metaphors. She may not actually know what she thinks she knows. This is a hard realization. When she figures this out, she may be upset. Finding out you misunderstand so much is harsh and painful. She needs you—and she needs mentors—to be there for her, to help her understand without making her feel like she fails for just not knowing.

Some days are going to be hard. Some days she may have fewer skills than others. *This is more distressing for her than it is for you.* Do not lose sight of this. It sucks to not know what your own capabilities are from day to day. It will not help her to fall into "woe" mode. It is not about you. She isn't trying to upset you. It is harder to experience this than to watch someone experience it. Keep sight of who this is actually about—your daughter. Stay calm when you can and go into the next room or even for a drive when you can't. Love her. She needs love from her parents, not yet another person she can't quite please, not yet another therapist. Do your best to understand and internalize that her inconsistent skills are not personal, and that they're bothering and inconveniencing her far more than you. If this is inaccurate, if they're bothering you more, you really need to take a step back. Do not appropriate her challenges but help her move through them.

Her needs are real, even if they are inconsistent. If she is stimming, it is a need. She *needs* that input. If she does better with visual supports, honor that. She trusts you and wants to please you. Be worthy of this honor. Do not abuse this trust with expectations that she do things that are impossible for her. Don't ask her to do things that take more energy from her than they are worth. Honor her needs. There is no great virtue in sitting still or remembering to do everything without visuals or in being able to be spontaneous. Do not violate her trust by convincing her there is. She deserves the truth, and the truth is that meeting her needs matters more than the performance of normal. There are no "grown-up police" who will go around making sure no one uses more than five sticky notes a week. Teach her that her needs matter more than the arbitrary "shoulds" from others.

I want you to know that you have been given an amazing gift in the form of your daughter, and a stunning responsibility. Life trusts you with a unique, beautiful soul. Your challenge is to raise her to know herself and her needs and to feel worthy of having her needs met. These are daunting tasks. I don't believe that special people are preordained to have special kids; that's about seven kinds of insulting-to-everyone nonsense. I do believe, however, that our parents can choose to become extraordinary.

Your girl deserves extraordinary. Break the mold. Make the decision that she *is* exactly the child you always dreamed of. Fiercely fight for her right to be an Autistic person. Love her dearly exactly as she is and raise her to know that she is perfect and that her needs are her rights. Be amazed at all the expectations an Autistic girl who already knows she pleases the most important adults in her life can shatter.

When the basic need to secure her parents' love is accomplished? She is free to take risks of failure, and so amaze you when she succeeds. Choose her. Allow her to shine. You won't regret it.

5 What I Wish You Knew

Katie Levin

I wish my parents knew that when I was refusing to do something, it was often because I was overwhelmed and wasn't given the right kind of support.

JUST BECAUSE I MAY BE well-behaved, quiet, and getting good grades at school doesn't mean that school is going well, or that I am not experiencing problems, or that I am happy.

I was smart, got good grades, and mostly tested well, but I was often afraid to ask questions in class. The worst thing was when the teacher asked us to "pick a partner" or a group, where everyone just usually paired up with someone right away. Since I was too afraid to ask anyone (and no one ever asked me), I was almost always one of the leftovers. That meant I was the kid who didn't have a partner and got thrown with whichever other kid didn't have a partner or thrown in someone's group of the teacher's choosing as an extra person. I was too scared to call most kids on the phone or walk with anyone. When I was in junior high and I took the bus to school, I waited alone at the bus stop because I was too scared to ask anyone if I could wait with them.

I needed the support of a special education environment, but not the remedial level work. I often mainstreamed out of special education because I was too smart. It wasn't fair that smart kids couldn't get the extra support of a special education environment, and when I was mainstreamed into harder classes, I often had a hard time keeping up with the work. Plus, special education kids are judged by other kids. It was either/or: harder work with not enough support, or more support with work that was too easy. I couldn't have both the work at the level that was right for me and the extra support I needed.

I hated gym class more than anything. I was uncoordinated, not very fast or strong, and afraid of balls coming toward me. The teacher never offered to help me learn whatever we were doing or improve any skills, or even showed encouragement or support. The other kids never wanted me to be on their team (I was always picked last, again a "leftover"). They just ignored me or yelled at me whenever I was stuck on someone's team because I never did well. I hated that I was forced to participate against my will. I sometimes wore the wrong shoes on purpose so I could sit out and not play in elementary school.

For similar reasons, I didn't often enjoy recess. I would walk around by myself or play on the swings alone unless someone offered to play with me (which usually didn't happen). Most kids ignored me, but some teased me and bullied me. I almost always started to cry whenever that happened, and that just overwhelmed me even worse than their teasing.

I got overwhelmed in large groups. I got invited to a few birthday parties, but not many. I never had more than four people come to any of my birthday parties. Many times I had only two or three.

What was worse was that even when my parents fought to give me more support (special classroom, special school and resources), the school system usually voted against it. It wasn't until the end of my freshman year of high school, after being hospitalized twice in eighteen months, that the school finally pulled me from mainstream placement and placed me in special education. There were two problems with this. One was that all the work was remedial level and too easy for me, and the second was that I was placed in the behavior disorder or BD class with all the kids who were suspended regularly and usually dropped out of school before graduating. I was the kid who was naive, smart, never got a detention in my life, and was afraid of just about everyone. So, I was placed with a bunch of bullies.

I wish my parents knew that when I was "refusing" to do something, it was often because I was overwhelmed and wasn't given the right kind of support, especially when it came to chores. It was also difficult to be around a bunch of people, and in asking if we could go to a different (quieter) restaurant, or turn off certain noises, or not give Grandma a kiss and a hug all the time, I wasn't trying to be rude. These were sensory issues. My parents often told me I needed to learn to "get over it," and if I didn't, I'd never be able to function in life, college, on the job, with a boyfriend, etc.

I wish I could have grown up in an environment where I wasn't constantly treated like I was broken. I felt like I wasn't okay unless I learned to act like everyone else. I realized later on that my mom sent me to therapists partly thinking that they would instruct me in doing whatever my mom said. After all, my parents were the ones paying the therapist.

I also want today's parents to know that I noticed the examples of others' actions more than their yelling or punishments. If you tell me to clean up, even though your room and other parts of the house are a mess, it's not going to help me to learn the skill. If you're telling me to do something just because you told me so (and if I don't, I'll be punished), I will grow up to resent wanting to help you with anything. And in many ways that is what happened.

Kids need to learn living skills while still young, even if they need help: how to do the laundry, how to wash the dishes, how to make a bed, how to cook, how to answer a phone, how to use public transportation, and—when they're old enough—how to drive. They might need your help and support, maybe multiple times. They need you to be *patient*. Don't yell if they do something wrong, even if they do it wrong one hundred times.

Girls can show autism differently than boys do. Girls may not act out as much. They might be more verbal. We are often taught not to be as physical, but to be more social. We might not have the more common autistic interests like video games or trains. We are judged more on our social skills and our looks. We often learn to suppress anything that is out of the ordinary, like unusual special interests or stimming or unusual habits.

It's okay to get a diagnosis. Getting a diagnosis doesn't define you or your child. You and your child choose what they want to do with it. It might help them get certain accommodations such as extended test times at college or government benefits. But it's not always relevant. And once your child is diagnosed, they can learn more about autism, and why they shouldn't feel like they are broken and how to navigate the world around them, even if their mind works differently.

Three things:

- Your child loves you even if they don't always show it.
- Make sure your child's special talents are recognized and encouraged.
- Teach your child to learn to use their strengths to compensate for their so-called deficits or struggles.

If at all possible, try to limit the amount of homework your child gets. Being in school for seven hours a day is mentally exhausting. That includes recess and lunch. Being in school is all about following rules and acting appropriately. We have to constantly remember all these rules. School is all about acting like everyone else. We often have to put on a persona that is outside of our comfort zone. And we usually can't take breaks when we want. When we get home, we need a chance to get away from that. We can't be expected to act this way 24/7. If we are, we are more likely to become overwhelmed faster, shut down more frequently, act out in destructive ways, become physically ill more often, become depressed, and avoid social situations.

Let us stim, especially at home. It might seem awkward to do this at school, especially since other kids will often judge it. If it's not destructive and it isn't harmful, let us get it out of our system. If the behaviors are bothersome to others, show your child where they can do this in private or leave the room for a while to allow your child to do this.

Being happy is not the same as being normal. We just want to be accepted.

6 Change the World, Not Your Child

Lei Wiley-Mydske

This is your child's humanity, their disabled humanity, and it is important.

GROWING UP, I wish my parents had known that teaching me to fight for my rights was more important than forcing me to fit in. I was conditioned early to know that my saying "no" was not an option, certain "atypical" behaviors needed to be eliminated, and being compliant made me "good." I spent a lot of time learning to deny my natural impulses and feelings in order to conform to what was expected of a "good girl." In doing so, I opened myself up to become a victim of both emotional and sexual abuse from adults and intense bullying from my peers. The way I experienced the world around me was supposedly wrong, and there was no argument. So, I remained silent. Always.

I am not writing this to blame my parents for the abuse I endured at the hands of others, because I honestly believe that they did the best that they could. Forty years ago, little was known about autism, and even less about how autism was experienced by girls and women. Now we know better. Now we have a vibrant community of Autistic activists and self-advocates who are stepping up to tell you what autism really is. We are pushing back. We are fighting for our rights and the rights of your Autistic children. When society tells us that our lives are not valuable, we need the people who love us to stand with us and shout back, "You are WRONG!"

As the parent of an Autistic child, you cannot afford to be neutral. I'm not saying that you have to pick up a sign and start protesting the Judge Rotenberg Center (a residential school for disabled students known for its abusive disciplinary tactics) or start volunteering for a disability rights organization (though that would be great). What I am saying is that your child cannot afford for you to hold back when taking a stand for their rights.

Your child is Autistic. Your child is disabled. These are not negative things. These things just are. The way this world is going to treat your child, well, that's another story. Society views disabled lives with pity, contempt, and fear.

Do you want your child to live in a world where that's okay? Or do you want to stand up, be an ally, and fight until your child's humanity and dignity are deemed just as important as a non-disabled person's humanity?

That might sound scary—asking you to fight. And it can be scary, I know that.

The question you need to ask yourself is, "Is my child worth it?"

I promise you, the answer is always "yes."

This is your child's humanity, their disabled humanity, and it is important.

No one expects one person to change the entire world. What you can do is change *your* world. You can give your child the tools to be a strong self-advocate. You can give your child an example of a true ally by changing the conversation about autism and disability in your own lives and homes.

How do you do that?

Presume competence. Presume that your child is aware and wants to understand. Consider that this may look different than what you expect. Assume that when your child is having a hard time, that your child is actually having a hard time. They are not being lazy, or manipulative, or trying to make your day worse. Accommodations and supports are *not* excuses.

Respect your child. Do not do to your Autistic child what you would not do to a typically developing child. Your Autistic child is not in need of fixing. They are in need of acceptance and understanding. Your child gets only *one* childhood. Remember that. Therapies that value compliance and normalcy or sameness amongst peers are not respectful of your child's dignity, individuality, and autonomy. They are setting the stage for how others are allowed to treat your child. If you value compliance over autonomy, your child will likely learn to be compliant and more vulnerable.

Redefine normal. Recognize that normal is subjective. Stimming, flapping, perseverance, and accommodating sensory preferences are not reasons to apologize. Your job is to build your child up, not tear them down due to a stranger's disapproving glare. Never apologize for your child being openly Autistic.

Calm down. Your Autistic child at three is not your Autistic child at nine. Or at fifteen or thirty. Do not write the story of your child's life before they even enter kindergarten. We all develop in our own time, in our own way. This knowledge can save you many headaches. This does not mean that every Autistic child is going to grow up and live independently. I would argue that *nobody* lives independently. We are all interdependent, some more than others. In my own life, I have never been truly able to live alone or without support. I cannot drive. I even have a hard time not getting lost on the bus. I still have a good quality of life because I am surrounded by people who respect me as a person, accommodate me, and who do not define me by my deficits.

Seek out the Autistic community. Autistic adults are here, and we have been where your child has been. Our experiences are all different and varied. Yet every single one of us knows what it is like to live an Autistic life in a world that is hostile to our neurology. If you want to learn about autism and what it is like to live an Autistic life, no one else will be able to help you understand like we can. Do not discount our voices.

Lastly, understand what acceptance really means. It does not mean no supports or accommodations. It does not mean no help or therapies. Acceptance means that you accept your child's Autistic neurology as valid. It means understanding that the way your child experiences the world is uniquely Autistic. Acceptance means embracing the amazing Autistic person that your child is. Our children deserve to be loved for exactly who they are, with all their strengths and all their weaknesses. Your love and acceptance for your child should never be conditional on how well they can "perform" as non-Autistic.

When we value Autistic and disabled lives, we understand that love and acceptance are critical. This idea is not controversial when raising allistic children. When it comes to Autistic lives, however, we get frightening messages that who we are is broken and that we need to be fixed. Do not get caught up in those messages of fear. This is why I say that you must take a stand for your child's rights. Your child deserves to be seen as a whole and complete human being who is worthy of the same rights as everyone else.

A child who is raised by parents who presume competence and who treat them with dignity is a child who is strong. When we allow children to develop in their own time frame, in their own ways, and allow them to be their own unique selves along the way, we are telling our children that who they are is valuable. We are telling our children that they are worthy of respect, that their Autistic lives might be different, but that differences can and should be celebrated. When we choose acceptance and love over fear, we are teaching our children that they can make this world a better place. They already have, just by being who they are.

7 Empathy and Non-Verbal Cues

Dusya Lyubovskaya

No matter how young your child is, your child understands their surroundings better than you think!

━━━━━━━

I AM NOT SURE how exactly to start.

I am now an adult in my thirties, and I was diagnosed when I was in my late twenties.

Although my mother never knew until recently that I have Asperger's, and although my grandparents (who passed away over twenty years ago) never knew that I have Asperger's, both my mother and my grandparents always loved and accepted me despite my quirks.

If I got upset or if I was confused, my mother, grandmother, or grandfather would patiently explain to me until I would calm down, and I am very thankful for that.

I think I learned a lot about patience from my grandparents.

Since I was a child, I have been very intuitive in terms of my observations of a situation. I would often tell my mother or my father that either something was going to go wrong or that I had a bad feeling.

At first, my mother was surprised, but after a couple of incidents, my mother always appreciated my observations, and it did not matter to her that I was a child at the time my so-called sixth sense started. My father, on the other hand, did not want to listen to whatever I had to say, unfortunately, because he was stuck with the notion that I was a child and that children do not know or cannot understand anything.

I have no intention of blaming my father for his reactions, although I am perhaps making that impression. I am simply sharing my memories and experiences here. I have forgiven him because I realize that he simply did not know better.

Because of my father's reactions, throughout the years I stopped paying attention to my intuitive senses because I felt ridiculed.

It has now been a couple years since my father passed away, and as I have mentioned, I have forgiven him. And the beauty of forgiving him is that I am learning to pay attention to my senses again.

The reason I am talking about this is that I want to reach out to other parents and ask them to please pay attention to what your child communicates.

No matter how young your child is, your child understands their surroundings better than you think!

I understand if parents think, "What could my autistic child possibly understand?"

Well, my response is that your autistic child is very intelligent and even if your autistic child is not able to communicate verbally, your child will communicate in other ways, like writing a letter to you or a poem or typing something on the computer. Your child can communicate!

And just listen to what your child says. Even if it does not make sense to you, have a conversation with your child; your child needs to know that you are taking them seriously. Discuss with your child their feelings to find out why they are thinking or feeling a certain way.

Another issue that I struggled with was that because I had difficulty verbalizing my thoughts and needs, I did not like and was irritated when adults made assumptions about why they thought I was crying.

Instead of asking what was wrong or if I wanted a glass of water or any other thing that I could have had, they instead made assumptions, guessed, or had already made up their minds about why I was crying.

For example, I remember when I was six or seven years old, for some reason I was not interested in looking at babies. Well, let me be clearer about this: I liked children between two and six years old, but newborns or older babies I did not like, and I did not want to look at them, either. (I still have no explanation for this.)

So, when I was six years old and taking a walk with my mother, a woman who lived on the next block approached us and showed us her newborn, and I started crying and this woman thought that I was jealous, and I was not able to communicate that I just did not find babies that exciting.

Nowadays, I still do not find them exciting, but I do not mind looking at them. I am willing to hold a baby, but I do not feel like gushing at one.

Generally, I just wish that adults, who in this case were strangers, would've asked me why I was crying, or at least told my mother to ask me. I think that it would have been easier for me to learn how best to cope with sensory issues if adults would have asked me questions instead of making constant assumptions.

If adults would have asked me questions, and been creative with their questions, I could have better learned to cope with my sensory issues, and I would not be ashamed of them or embarrassed by them.

So now, I still have to learn to cope, like understanding why I am having a meltdown, and I am learning that I have meltdowns because I do not feel comfortable in an environment or because I need help because I am frustrated and not able to communicate that I am frustrated.

Nowadays, it is like a guessing game for me, and it frustrates me as well, because I strongly believe that if I'd had adults interested in listening to me and asking me questions as opposed to making assumptions, my life as an adult would be much easier. That is for sure!

8 The First Time I Heard of Autism

Anonymous

The possibility of your darling child being autistic doesn't mean they're flawed or less amazing.

AS SOMEONE WHO IS as closely involved with the autistic community as I am, I wish I could say that the first time I heard the word or concept of autism was a positive one. But it wasn't, and yet it came from my mother, who worked as a school counselor of all things.

When I was a young child in the 1990s (or the late 1900s, if I want to make all of us feel old), my mother was taking grad school classes and would sometimes take me along due to a lack of available childcare, and I'd play alone in some nearby empty classroom.

One of those times, I met a boy my age who was in the same boat, waiting for his grad student mom to get out of class. He struck me as strange because he wouldn't talk, but he had building blocks, and we sat to play together. After all, children make friends easily. We played for a while without ever exchanging words.

After some time, my mother got out of class and took me with her. She was all worried and asked me if that kid had hurt me in any way and said that I should stay away from him because he's "so and so's kid" and he was autistic.

At the time I had no idea what that term meant, only that it was clear that my mother somehow thought the quiet child with building blocks I had just spent time with was somehow bad or dangerous.

Later in adulthood, as I came to realize my own autistic identity, I learned just how many people's "radars" I had set off, and how many people around me in childhood had suspected it. After my mother's tragic passing, I learned from my relatives that she had been encouraged to get me assessed for autism, but she refused to do so. To be fair, she only expected perfection from her one and only child. I was gifted, she thought, and I would change the world.

So, this prompts the question: What is it that I wish my parents knew about autism? Well, the basic fact that we aren't evil, or dangerous, or something to be feared. That we're not violent. That the possibility of your darling child being autistic doesn't mean they're flawed or less amazing.

Likewise, that having a math learning disability doesn't mean that you're somehow "dumb" or "stupid," even if you're good at everything else.

Of course, the true confrontation with my mother came about because of my gender identity and sexuality, which is what I truly wish she had understood—that being trans isn't dooming yourself to a life of hardship and misery, or a choice to spite her, or, least of all, her fault. Maybe, had I been recognized as autistic, it would have been either easier or harder. I do not know. It took me until I was in my twenties to finally reach what I'd refer to as a "Korean Peace"—armistice and cessation of armed conflict without a peace treaty.

9 What I Wish My Parents Knew About Being Their Autistic Daughter

Heidi Wangelin

I feel strongly about things, but I can't always say it. ▬▬▬

BEING AUTISTIC is kind of an unusual thing, especially since I am an Autistic woman who, while growing up, was the only Autistic girl I knew, which was kind of lonely and confusing. I was diagnosed as Autistic when I was six years old at the University of Michigan Ann Arbor, and what I mostly remember about this experience was that I was intensely fixated on peeling the Michigan lighthouse calendar off the wall, amused with watching it fall, and looking at all the pictures. I really liked the colors, especially the blues and whites, and the crashing waves. The graduate student was busily taking notes on a stool and looking a bit annoyed at me because I was still fiddling with the calendar, which would drop down to the seat and slip through the cracks and sometimes land on my head. I knew my mom was getting annoyed, too, and wanted me to stay still. I was never the kid who liked staying still, and that could be a problem. The chair was green-backed and metal, and I was about to fall off. The wall was white and kind of bumpy. Then the student cleared his throat and told my mom I was Autistic. My mom nodded and asked about what it meant. I still was playing with the calendar. I didn't realize how dramatically my life would change after this ordeal.

For the next several years, I lacked a sense of stability. I was constantly forced into the role of being the new kid with every school change, and it was always hard to adjust. Five consecutive moves are a lot for one person to go through, and it never helped that, as I stated earlier, I was the only Autistic girl I knew. I did make friends with each place I moved to, and I still keep in touch with a few of them now, but I still get lonely. I think the worst part of school, especially as someone who moved frequently, was that I often didn't know where I'd sit at lunch. I really liked to read and made friends easily, but unfortunately most of the time it was with the teachers, since I liked learning. I also used to edit my classmates' papers during study hall because it was easy for me to have something to correct. I learned how to read everyone's spelling tests, and it was actually kind of fun for me to play the role of editor. My math work was always terrible, though, and still is.

Sometimes I wish I could tell my parents now what I felt as both a kid and as an adult. Growing up, I tried to write everything. One night I threw parts of my writing into a bonfire pit in a fit of anger because I was frustrated at a friend who had upset me. Watching it burn felt good, but unfortunately, being lonely couldn't be solved just by burning a piece of paper. Anger is a funny thing, and I was more of a crier anyway. I suppose I felt moving was like that, too—being ripped away from what I knew—but there was no way to say that. I often found it frustrating that I could get along better with a piece of paper or a teacher than with another student. I still have this issue now, and I can revert to this kind of thinking even as an adult.

Water has also been a constant source of both sensory input and comfort, since it felt good to have it splash across my face and legs. If I had my way, I'd always be in water. Water and a piece of paper won't let you down like people do, and you can always erase the paper somehow. You can't erase people from your life as easily, and having a photographic and episodic memory makes it even more challenging to forget someone. The memory of a person always comes back to me somehow. Sometimes I didn't want to erase people, but I just didn't know how to deal with it. So instead, I'd shut down. It wasn't like I never tried to be social and make friends; I've just never been good at it and settled for what was easy—not because I wanted to, but because I was just tired. When you are tired, sometimes you resort to odd tactics to cope.

Knowing I was the only Autistic girl at school was like having a birthmark or something distinct that everyone could see. Sometimes I liked it, as though it were a cool feature, like my pretty brown eyes. But other times I hated it, kind of like my awkward chest. Looking back, I think most of my hate was just me being frustrated.

Loneliness was the hardest part of growing up, more than any bullying ever was. Looking back now, as I write this in my new apartment with my little desk all messed up and staring out into the tree planter, I think much of my loneliness was self-imposed. I often thought that most people didn't like me. I knew my parents loved me and that my teachers liked me, but I honestly believed that people my own age disliked me. I also struggled with depression, and even though the medication sometimes helped, I felt like I was losing control of myself, like I didn't know who I was.

I like to think in pictures and sounds like a camera, so it was like having a rush of feelings and pictures coming straight into my eyes and brain, and I couldn't find the words to describe it. At times it is like a camera that I can't control, though. Certain things will set off my camera, and I can't always process feelings when this happens. It is called being alexithymic, or not being able to say and think your emotions at the same time they are being experienced. This is what always gets me stuck and unable to talk. I know it frustrates my mom when I can't speak about what I'm feeling or make decisions. It's just as frustrating for me.

In addition, I feel like I often pick up on others' feelings with my internal camera. Feelings can be overpowering for me, too, being an empathetic person. I really hate picking up others' feelings, because they become my own; I can't block them out even if I try. If someone is hurting, for me it is overpowering; it feels like being stabbed in the gut. Or if someone is happy, I can feel it, too. I can also sense feelings of anger and sadness easily, even other people's pain. I can't read body language well, but I can feel things pretty strongly.

The only times that I am able to block out my own feelings is if I'm in survival mode. When that happens, I shut down so much that I can turn off my facial expressions. Unfortunately, that also means that my thoughts get turned off, too. When this happens, it doesn't always hit me right in the moment, but sometimes much later. I feel strongly about things, but I can't always say it. And sometimes what looks like a meltdown is really just an expression that I'm upset, but those feelings came out in a meltdown. It's not always what it looks like. Parents, please be aware that your child may feel this too.

In high school, I also hated that I was always considered "one of the guys" even though I'm a woman. I'm not the most feminine person around, but I'm not all masculine either. I like my blazers and button-downs, old sweaters, and old shirts and jeans. But I have long hair and I also like dresses. I don't wear makeup often, and until last year I always wore glasses that looked like my dad's. Autism sometimes feels like an old boys' club after a while, and it gets frustrating being the only girl around. I don't have a "male brain," either—another silly theory. And it sucks having to adjust each outfit to make sure I can be taken seriously.

Each person is different and sometimes people call me not autistic enough or too autistic. Most of these people were autistic themselves, so that makes it seem even more silly to me. There's no such thing as being too autistic or not. How can we measure someone's degree of autism? Why would we want to? Parents, don't fall into the same trap while socializing your child, thinking they're "too" autistic. Would you measure yourself on what kind or degree of parent you are?

It's important to constantly push back against sexism and ableism. Because this starts when we are very young, many of us grow up thinking that is normal or acceptable. This is a horrible lie that we've been told, and it needs to stop. Part of why I liked having a joint major in Disability Studies is because it allowed me a place to discuss this kind of thing. I guess you can call it one of my obsessions. It isn't the most popular obsession out there, though, since it can really make people angry to be called out on disability issues and since I get lots of confused looks from others.

Neurodiversity, the belief that all brains are needed and can be beautiful, is something I wish I had learned about sooner. It isn't any different than biodiversity—the variance of life—except that it has to do with brains. Parents, tell your child that their brain is beautiful. From being around neurotypicals, I have spent most of my life thinking that I wasn't enough. I felt that I had to aspire to be a neurotypical most of my life. That attitude was wrong, and I was only harming myself.

Tell your children they are wanted. Often, we Autistics are shown that we aren't wanted. We need each other, both neurotypicals and Autistics. I know that it can be scary to embrace being Autistic or that your child is autistic. Take time to process, but don't grieve. Grief is like wishing your child away.

If I had an opportunity to talk to younger me (little Heidi), I would reassure her that she is going to be just fine. She's not broken, just different—a good kind of different. Do you have a little Heidi in your life? She needs you. She wants you to know how it feels, and please don't judge her. What are you most proud of about her? What is she most proud of?

Tell little Heidi that she is beautiful, just like you. Respect her autonomy. She's a person. She's not a thing or less than human. She is like you somehow. Too often, people with disabilities in general are treated as less than people. Let her get involved in her passions and be part of the disability rights movement if she is inclined to that kind of passion. We need more representatives who are autistic. We need you and her. We need you to understand us. Accept us as people. She may have a different way of showing what she feels and needs, but it is important. I am blessed to have mostly understanding parents, but not everyone is as lucky or privileged as I am.

Tell her that she's not alone, that there are more people just like her. I think the biggest issue for me was feeling alone. I didn't meet any women my age who were Autistic and proud of it until my sophomore year of college. I think if I'd had more Autistic female role models, that would have helped me a lot. I'm excited every time I am able to mentor others, especially young people. I have a chance to be the role model that I never had. I can help people—like your child!—to embrace who they are, know they matter, know they're not alone. I hope this helps you understand.

10 A Particular Way of Being

Karen Lean

Allow your daughter to veer off whatever map you think she's been placed on
——

TEACH YOUR GIRL to be fierce instead of delicate. Trash gender expectations and nurture the child in front of you. Refuse to be typical parents, because your child is not typical. Refuse the status quo, because it does not serve girls and it especially does not serve autistic girls.

Girls should get dirty. We should ask questions and explore. We need our anger, our curiosity, our boundaries, our softness, our toughness, our brilliance. We need to learn that we're not wrong merely because we don't match our peers or our gender or those autism textbooks. We can be powerful if you help us remove the obstacles in our way. We deserve confidence in our powers as birthrights.

Autistic girls mess up norms. We bust misconceptions about gender and autism. These are assets in spite of a world that thinks otherwise. Don't expect girls to labor under the burdens of wrong expectations. Instead, nurture possibility and difference.

I object to the term "disorder" for describing autism. I object to that description overall because autism has a coherence. It's certainly a different way of experiencing the world, but the problem and the dis-order happens because non-autistic people aren't listening to actual autistics.

By different I don't mean special, and I rather despise the term "special needs." By different, I mean that many people I talk to do not identify with my experience even if they can understand it. Many people do not, and have no interest in, understanding. I hope that as a parent of a girl labeled as some kind of autistic, you have an interest in understanding.

Listen to your girl. Even if she doesn't talk, she's telling you something.

Sensory Experiences

I don't usually cheer about psychiatry, but I cheered when the American Psychological Association included sensory differences in the *DSM-5* criteria for autism spectrum disorder. It's a step in the right direction because I think that the sensory and neurological landscape of autistics is central to understanding autism.

I feel intensely. I smell mold and bad food before others. I hear fluorescent lights. Clothing hurts, noises invade, colors take my breath away. My daily reality is governed by too much sensation and not enough sensation. Patterns are soothing because they create order in what feels like chaos. Sometimes I shut down and I lose language. Other times I get overloaded and act it out in ways that get me in trouble. My world is intense, rich, real, sometimes painful, and definitely different.

Understand the sensory experience of your child by being curious. Establish her as the authority in this experience. Do not question it but instead ask questions: "Wow, the clouds have lots of colors in them? Can you tell me more about them? Can you name them?" If she's using her body in ways you don't understand, let her explain. If she can't tell you, try to think about what she may be gaining from doing this. I usually do things like wiggle my hands or tap on my head in private because I learned it wasn't okay to do it in public. I now see that these kinds of repetitive behaviors are methods of calming. Research supports this view, and I think we need to facilitate self-regulation. Even the most socially unacceptable behavior likely has a purpose. She deserves your help being creative so that she can meet her needs.

Understand your girl's sensory world and honor her experience as fiercely as you honor gravity. If you deny your child's desires and pain around her sensory world, she may learn that her body and boundaries are not worth respecting.

As a child I learned that my body and my boundaries were wrong. I learned that my discomfort couldn't possibly be real because my discomfort was uncommon. For example, if my parents put me in a shirt that had a rough tag, I learned that if I cried no one would understand that the clothing hurt me. I felt dismissed when I talked about it, and I was a compliant child, so I didn't take off the offending item. I learned to put up with extreme bodily discomfort. Relent to pain often enough and it doesn't become less painful; it becomes a lesson that the pain doesn't matter. I started to distrust my own body. Almost forty years later, I tolerate discomfort that I should put a stop to.

The pain doesn't disappear into the background. It interferes with being curious and present in the world. Sensory pain is distracting—I pay less attention to social cues when my senses are overburdened. This kind of overburdening affects my social perception and communication. For instance, when I wear a comfortable outfit to work, I focus better, I think more clearly, and I am more effective with people.

Rather than take issue with wearing the same clothing every day, find out what works about that clothing and buy more of it. Let your girl wear clothes that are comfortable even if they're boy-gendered; you can find crafty ways to feminize them if that's what she wants. If you emphasize her appearance as more important than her well-being, she will likely learn that what other people think about how she looks is more important that who she is or how she feels.

Take the distractions and discomforts of her body seriously and help your girl address the worst offenders through creativity. One of the most powerful tools you can give her is control over her environment, her attention, and her physical comfort.

Sensory experiences can range from very painful to highly pleasurable. Understand this and teach your child how to communicate about her pain and pleasure so that she learns how to self-regulate it. Teach her how to understand boundaries around pleasure and pain.

Parents, I hate to tell you this: I strongly connect disrespecting my sensory boundaries with a vulnerability to unwanted sexual contact. Kids must learn to read cues about whether their actions are wanted or not and respect that communication. When they don't, they are doing something wrong and the consequences can lead to a pattern of harming people. Kids also need to learn to communicate about unwanted actions that involve their bodies, minds, and hearts. When we don't, the consequences can lead to a pattern of allowing ourselves to be harmed.

Autistic girls may have the additional challenges of compromised sensory boundaries and freeze and overwhelm reactions. Sometimes I completely shut down and could not stop what was happening with words or actions. I did have sex education, and I learned what was appropriate and inappropriate, but I didn't understand what *felt* unsafe until I was so unsafe that I froze.

We need to understand what we don't want and then communicate clearly, unapologetically, and with enough force to stop it. We need the skills to fight for our integrity. However, even with these skills, we are still vulnerable if our sensory world isn't made safe, because we won't understand what safety feels like. Sexual safety means nothing if we ignore our most basic needs for sensory safety.

Encourage your girl to push her boundaries in positive ways, but teach her to never let anyone encroach on her personal space or tell her that she's weak for experiencing the world the way she does.

Honor her "NO" every single time.

Learning from Mistakes

I choose not to focus on my strengths or my weaknesses. Do you try to focus on her strengths and not her weaknesses in the interest of her self-esteem? Perhaps you experience her weakness as what challenges you, and her strength as what pleases you. I can understand this, but I urge you to turn these on their head for a moment. Maybe they are difficult because you don't understand her needs around them. What if her needs are perfectly reasonable and when they're met on their own terms, she can grow as she will? What if you encouraged her to fail? I became a perfectionist because I felt I got the most love and attention for what I did well. I didn't feel like I could fail and still be loved. I was terrified of disappointing my parents and teachers. I was allowed to give up if things were too difficult. Worse, I rarely attempted something that was hard. I don't believe anyone did harm to me on purpose, but I developed an intense aversion to challenge.

Work to understand what your girl struggles with and encourage those struggles. Whether they are social, academic, or physical mistakes, encourage exploration.

I hid my struggles by focusing exclusively on what I did well and did myself a disservice in the process: People assume I do not have challenges in some areas because I am competent in others. Just because I can write a successful grant proposal doesn't mean I can navigate a crowded club to stay safe. Just because I can explain how matrilineal descent works doesn't mean I can figure out what to order from a restaurant menu. Just because I can be really articulate and give a television interview doesn't mean I am able to speak up when I'm emotionally distressed or threatened.

I learned that people won't believe me when I say I need help, and so I stopped asking. I found passive or covert ways of getting help, which ultimately led to poor self-advocacy. I learned helplessness. Seeking assistance in these ways is highly ineffective and even harmful in adulthood. It has led to relationship dynamics I'm not proud of.

I realized I was different from my peers in grade three. I remember being teased and that this is the first year I can recall being depressed. Grade three is when Sally told me to stop liking Jane because Jane was being mean to Sally, and I thought, "Why would I stop liking Jane when she did nothing to me?" I now understand that all of these types of friendship dynamics were practice for an increasingly complex social world that I didn't grasp then.

Autistic girls may be able to mimic certain aspects of play and social skills, but the learning curve in the girl world is steep. The school held me back from the gifted stream, and I attribute these social and emotional difficulties to why I remained unchallenged in school. By sixth grade I was isolated, kids bullied me, and I was so depressed that my parents helped me find another school—luckily, I got into an arts program that helped me flourish.

In the 1980s, there was no label for my particular constellation of genius-level academics and social lagging. I was a model student: shy and gawky, with a few friends. Getting into an arts-focused school enabled me not only to express myself through artistic outlets, but to find peers who were more like me.

If your girl has particular interests that can be nourished through any outlet, find it and help her pursue it. Recognize that her peers may not be the kids on her street or in her school—or even her age. If she gets along better with an adult mentor, facilitate that.

I didn't grow up with a label and imagine that being diagnosed as a child can bring extra support but also limitations. I spoke with someone at the Asperger/Autism Network[1] who told me that a school-age girl with my profile (strong academics, sensory issues hidden, socially behind but behaviorally compliant) would still be overlooked for an autism spectrum diagnosis.

I sought a diagnosis at thirty-two, after years of struggle. I hit suicidal lows in graduate school, where the social demands of marriage and academics became too much for me. Every autistic woman is going to be unique, and the staffer told me that many girls today are identified as autistic in their teens when high school pressures become too much, or they disclose abuse, or enter the mental health system (perhaps they self-injure or have an eating disorder—things which commonly co-occur with autism). Not every girl who experiences these things is autistic, but the links are important. Don't compare autistic girls with boys or let any clinician or educator disregard how being autistic and female is a particularly challenging way to grow up.

Presume capacity.

Help her learn that her best qualities get that way by her hard work and persistence.

Don't let anyone tell your girl that she is wrong for being herself. Help her love who she is when she is playing or studying or flapping or spinning or singing or painting or drumming or bouncing or screaming or crying or finding beauty in the most unlikely places. You can show her you accept that she is exactly where she needs to be.

I am starting in my late thirties to finally love who I am. I challenge myself to grow, and I value my perceptions of the world. I have a great job in IT where I consistently learn new skills. I am discovering how be kind with myself and stop letting the world dictate how I need to be. When I speak in front of groups, I occasionally encounter a parent who will tell me how different I am from their child. The implication is that they don't believe I am autistic, or that perhaps they do not see their child becoming like me.

This closing thought is for parents like this (and if you've met me, you could be one of them):

Autistic women are engineers, mothers, farmers, artists, lawyers, activists, professors, welders, writers, chefs, gardeners, models, CEOs, advisors, knitters, singers, spinners, acrobats, poets, witnesses, lawmakers, locksmiths, and everything else. We have children at your school, and we are in your social club and your church. Allow your daughter to veer off whatever map you think she's been placed on and let her discover that who she is doesn't fit in any box—then celebrate that fact together.

Acceptance
and Adaptation

11 A Daughter's Journey: Lessons, Honesty, and Love

Jennifer St. Jude

She will forever be happy knowing she was loved enough that you are here fighting and advocating for her.

I WANT PARENTS and guardians of girls with autism to know that they will embark on many battles during this journey. Schools, healthcare needs, family relationships, etc., will repeatedly drag you into the advocacy arena. I want you to know that you will grow tired. You will have days when you feel like you've failed at everything. You will feel heartache at times watching your beautiful child suffer with her issues against the world. But while you will believe your child will only be happy when these things are all worked out, the truth is she will forever be happy knowing she was loved enough that you are here fighting and advocating for her. It's okay to make mistakes, to fail, to do everything the opposite way from what you planned for that day. It's okay to model saying "I'm sorry" more times than you can count. But when you end your day, end it knowing that you gave your child the most important thing she needed and longed for: your love and dedication!

I want parents and guardians to know that the fact that they are reading this and care about knowing and understanding more is evidence that they love and care deeply about their child. And *that* is something that matters more than anything else I say here.

Just as neurotypically developing boys and girls are different, boys and girls on the autism spectrum are also often very different. Thanks to many adult women on the spectrum who have grown up and returned to give our girls a voice, we now know that girls on the autism spectrum often manifest symptoms differently than boys do. We may "fake it" better because of our built-in social and communication advantages. So, while we may not be able to compete socially, we long to, try to, and pretend to. While we may not be able to truly express our hearts, we find ways to monologue, illustrate, and spell out our ideas and thoughts. Girls are often emotional and expressive by nature. When those pathways are interrupted by the delayed development of skills and abilities, a girl may feel a sense of quiet, and sometimes not so quiet, inner torment.

Today I am a mother of two daughters with autism, but I was also once a girl with autism myself. I deeply wanted to engage my peers and make connections as others did, but the map to them was beyond cryptic, if not altogether missing. The words I needed were buried in some language that I had not mastered at all. After I failed repeatedly and sometimes watched helplessly, I withdrew into my own private prison. I desperately studied humans and I later developed an "appropriate" monologue of responses and conversation starters. I found ways to look "normal" while inside I felt very far away from everyone. Through pattern seeking, I learned that people loved to talk about themselves and that I could be the grand listener. It served me and fooled many people into thinking I was doing well socially and had a lot of friends. But the truth was that as a teenager and young adult, I simply had a lot of pretend therapy clients. My covers were pulled off when adolescence brought on a cascade of emotions and problems for me to deal with myself. It was now my turn to seek the consolation of my peers and trusted adults. But that wasn't possible with my missing skills. Dealing with emotions and problems in adolescence requires a connection with others and is already quite challenging for anyone. Neurotypical girls survive by "talking out" their feelings and problems to their peers and trusted adults. I could not speak about my emotions or problems to anyone. This involved expressive organized speech, something in which I was weak and completely unpracticed. I also sometimes thought in pictures and emotional snippets, and my feelings had no words. I struggled to find scripts to accomplish expressing my feelings or troubles. But because these conversations are often private and hidden from bystanders, I couldn't watch others or copy them. Without the words to share my pain, and with no connections who could reach in and grab me, I grew silent and turned to drugs to comfort my anguished soul.

I learned the art of being an angry teen. Anger came easily for me, since meltdowns and frustration plagued me constantly, and I could now let it out. Anger required very little, if any, verbal expression. It also served to drive away those who desired to engage me in impossible conversations. Being intelligent but not fully functionally verbal, I was riddled with pride and struggled. Like all teens, I was in turmoil, but for me there was no way out. I did not see solutions or exits out of problems like others did. I did not collaborate with my peers to learn strategies to succeed. My constant struggle and heartache not only turned me to dangerous drug abuse, but I grew understandably suicidal. On the outside I appeared to be a quiet, occasionally explosive, unreasonable teen. I was "normal" in the eyes of adult outsiders expecting to see this in adolescents. Every passing year and my growing intelligence made it that much harder to confess to anyone the true reason for my strife and inner turmoil.

As I became an adult, I very slowly and painfully pieced together ways of coping. In the beginning I turned to addictions that only band-aided and then compounded my issues. After finding structure and support from twelve-step groups, I then began the difficult journey back to a connection with the world. I worked with many therapists, all of whom focused on verbal discussion to resolve issues. I tried really hard but couldn't use this method to get to anything. I was the hardest working person, getting nowhere, who I knew. The older I got, the more I was able to hide. I was driven into my own world. On the outside, I learned to monologue with comedy. People didn't expect me to have verbal communication skills when I was being funny and entertaining them. I could monologue my stories and experiences and others would just laugh or listen. I continued to gravitate to troubled souls, somewhat because I understood them and somewhat because they appreciated a listener who didn't talk. For years, I felt a bit like the Wizard in *The Wizard of Oz*. I was a frightened, trapped soul who used a big scary projection screen to scare off people in order to not get caught being vulnerable, lost, me. I could never ask for help because I didn't know what was wrong, nor did I know what help I even needed to ask for.

This continued for what felt like a lifetime. But it did have an end. In 2010, after discovering that I shared my daughters' autistic traits, I decided to get help. As my daughters' problems mounted and I could relate but not help them, I knew that I needed to do something fast. Getting my own help was the only chance my children had for me to be able to help them as well. I had to learn how to navigate me out of this mess if I was going to help them. They were beginning to cope and navigate the world better than I was, and encounter problems that I could not assist them with, because I had not learned those skills myself. I was so fortunate to stumble on the Autism Women's Network (now the Autistic Women & Nonbinary Network). There, on their website, my world began to grow, and more knowledge poured into me than I ever dreamed possible. I found hope again and was encouraged to find others just like me who had found their way to the world.

Eventually, I made an appointment and was evaluated for autism by the only therapist I knew of in Los Angeles who worked with adults. After being diagnosed with autism by a licensed clinical social worker, I began working in therapy with her. My world blew open and began to transform. I learned about my diagnosis and how to cope with it from my therapist, as well as attending a group for adult women with autism. I found meet-ups for adults with autism and an amazing community on Facebook, the Autism Discussion Page, which brilliantly illustrated "what to do now."[1] After years of being improperly diagnosed, I finally began to get the help and treatment I needed.

My anxiety issues were finally correctly diagnosed as sensory processing disorder, an issue that often co-occurs with autism. I started occupational therapy for my sensory processing disorder issues that were, by then, off the charts in intensity and crippling my life.

I could go on and list all my experiences, but regardless, every girl is different, and it might not always look for her as it looked for me. So, on the following pages are some basics that you need to know about your girl on the spectrum. And remember, when you feel completely stumped about an issue with your children, ask *them*. Let's face it, most people know themselves the best. Often, my daughters' ideas are brilliant and fresh. Consult the most experienced expert on your child; consult *her*.

Common Issues and Needs for Our Girls on the Autism Spectrum

ISSUES	NEEDS
Affection and Safe Contact	Our girls need the same connections to others, but sometimes need it differently. Explore ways of affectionately connecting with her (e.g., allow her to hug you, share a blanket, lean up against you, or just be in the same room as you).
	Children on the spectrum can sometimes be hyper-sexual. Teach her safe touch and rules for herself and others.
Asking for Help	*Will often not ask for help, not get their needs met, or be able to navigate initiating a conversation to ask for help.*
	Need scripts, phrases, and words that help them get their needs met and opportunities to learn to create their own scripts with help.
Boundaries	Can be an issue because she has not learned them easily via "non-verbal cues." She also might not notice others' poor boundaries.

ISSUES	NEEDS
Boundaries (cont.)	Give practical and tangible examples of boundaries (e.g., teach her that she should always stand at arm's length and ask people permission before touching them).
	Have good boundaries with her.
Cause and Effect	*People with Autism don't always see relationships between things.*
	Help her connect her behavior to the reactions of others and others' behavior to how it made her feel.
	When something positive happens, help her see the events that made it possible.
	When negative events reoccur, try and outline the possible causes (if any) so that she understands the connection.
Comfort	Getting comfort can be hard for our children. It is a social skill. She will need a "script" and a plan.
	Teach her how to ask for comfort and help her find ways that feel like comfort to her.
	Calming and grounding techniques are different for our kids. Explore her unique sensory needs and ways of comfort that are positive (e.g., no self-harm is acceptable).
Creativity	Allow your child to find her own creative way. Try lots of things and remind her that sometimes you have to find what you don't like to discover what you love.
Emotions	*Girls are emotional beings and emotions can be very difficult, especially when girls are diagnosed with Autism.*
	Adolescent girls with Autism struggle more with the world of emotions and are sensitive beings. Emotions don't always make sense or have the right timing. Remind them that it won't always feel this bad and that they are still learning.
	Tell them concrete stories of your own or those of other women with Autism so they don't feel so alone.
	Girls need to be taught the words for what they are feeling inside.

ISSUES	NEEDS
Emotions (cont.)	Teach her what she's feeling, then teach her how to express it (e.g., You seem angry, do you feel angry or mad? It's okay to tell me, "I feel really angry." If I know you are feeling angry, I can take time to listen to you and or give you the space you need and not make things worse.). Girls on the spectrum need to learn not only how to use words, but that they matter and make a difference in how others will treat them and experience them.
Empathy	Individuals with Autism are empathetic. However, "theory of mind" issues cause them to not understand what you are feeling to be able to respond. Once they know what you are feeling they then struggle to know how to respond appropriately. This often gets misunderstood as a "lack of empathy." Teach them how to ask people what they are feeling. Teach them how to respond to the different needs of others (e.g., "When someone says they are sick, ask them if they need anything and tell them you hope they feel better.").
Expressive and Receptive Speech	*Can hear okay but struggle with understanding what they hear and expressing thoughts and feelings.* Expressive: need to be taught concretely how to say things in a way that works and how to interpret and understand what others are saying. Receptive: teach them to ask people to speak more slowly. Teach them to check for understanding in both directions.
Friends, Belonging, and Connections	*Our girls desire to have friends, belong, and have connections (that feel good and aren't painful).* Need support and help in making friends by setting up play dates and educating other parents and their friends about what they might struggle with and how things can be better.

ISSUES	NEEDS
Friends, Belonging, and Connections (cont.)	Need help finding a place where they feel like they belong and fit. An Autism girls group, a meet-up, supportive Girl Scouts, a religious group, etc.
Frustration	*Frustration can get in the way of function. Emotions short-circuit the logical part of their brain. Girls feel emotions intensely and need calming strategies.* Make a list of soothing activities with your girl. If the list is short, then make a list of things to try and experiment with to see if she likes them. Always pair a difficult or new task with a preferred one that you know she likes.
Literal	*Individuals on the Autism spectrum are very literal.* Need information presented concretely. Speak literally and not figuratively for the best understanding. Help her see the message and not just the literal words.
Maturity	Girls mature faster and feel grown up in many areas while other areas remain very delayed. However, remember that your girl needs to be respected and consulted on matters that affect her. Teaching her how to handle difficult situations will help her mature.
Meltdowns	Meltdowns take on a different, more acceptable look as they grow older. They get moody, irritable, or angry. While these look like typical teen behaviors, it could be signs of early meltdown. Get a plan for this BEFORE it happens. Most importantly, remain calm yourself. When a human is in a state of meltdown they can't process information as easily.

ISSUES	NEEDS
Meltdowns (cont.)	Quietly and calmly remind her she is safe. Keep words small and slow.
Nurturing	Teach them self-nurturing by showing them and/or doing things with them (e.g., a facial, reading, warm baths, yoga, shopping, movies, cuddling, writing in a diary, art, projects, music, etc.). Teach them how to show caring for others with words and actions.
Obsessive Compulsive Disorder (OCD) and High Anxiety	Help ease her anxiety and OCD issues by consoling her worries and having her keep a journal of fears that she can write down answers you give her and helpful tips for feeling better. Creating a "plan" can really help ease anxiety. It can be a verbal list of activities for the day or a group of pictures like a comic layout.
Organization	Children with autism struggle with executive function skills. It makes it very difficult to do things in order and sometimes it's difficult to even get started. Help your child by teaching her organizational skills (e.g., using a calendar, setting reminders in her phone, making lists and checking-off items, even a picture schedule if it helps).
Practical	*Tasks need to make sense.* Need to understand when you ask them to do things different and how it will help. They can get stuck on the "Why?" Teach her that she may not see the reasons for a task but there are almost always reasons. Teach her acceptable ways to ask for explanations that don't get misunderstood as complaining (e.g., "I'm not complaining, I just need to understand why you need me to do this task. It's just how my brain works.").

ISSUES	NEEDS
Purpose	*Our girls desire to have purpose and to be of service in some way and have meaning in their lives.* Need to have a job or skill they do well so that they can feel good about themselves. Autism isn't all deficits!
Reasoning Skills	*Difficulty understanding the process of things. Girls on the spectrum are very concrete and very "here and now" in their thinking.* Help them to see the process of things by narrating things you do and why (e.g., I like to put my clothes out for the morning so that I don't have to think about it in the morning when I'm tired).
Responsibility	Sometimes our children struggle so much we don't want to burden them with more responsibility, but contributing (however small) increases self-esteem. Give your child a chore and help them succeed. Use charts, rewards, phone reminders.
Safety	Teach her specific words like "no" and "stop," and demonstrate them with her so she really understands their use. Show her by example by always respecting a girl's "no" and teach her that her "no" is important by honoring her words. Give her scripts to use in emergency situations and practice them. Create cards that speak for her in case she can't find the words. Role-play different emergency situations and have a solid plan. Keep safety plans and phone numbers of safe people in one place and make sure she can use them. Teach her how to dial 911 in an emergency and explain the reasons to call.

ISSUES	NEEDS
Seeing the "Big Picture"	*Individuals on the spectrum have difficulty seeing the larger view of things and tend to focus on the immediate details in front of them. This makes it difficult to plan or work toward things.*
	Creativity will collide with the Autistic rigid practical mind (e.g., a girl on the spectrum might get caught between wanting to draw but not see the purpose in it). Teach her that the purpose is in the moment and that it strengthens her brain and calms it.
	Help her to see the big picture by constantly stretching beyond her literal immediate moment of now (e.g., "I hang my clothes up right away so they don't get wrinkles and have to be ironed later.").
Sensitive and Empathic Beings	Girls on the spectrum are often sensitive and empathic to other people's emotions.
	Help her understand feelings of her own and interpret the feelings of others.
Sensory Processing Issues and Disorder	Seek help from an occupational therapist for sensory issues.
	They get overwhelmed with touch and other senses and experience a great deal of what seems to be anxiety, but it might be sensory processing issues.
	Teach her concrete ways and tools that will help her sensory system feel organized (e.g., stretching, deep-pressure massage, meditation, wrapping up in a stretchy blanket, etc.). Get help from an occupational therapist.
	Try some activities known to help organize the brain and nervous system, such as yoga, gymnastics, horseback riding, dance, volleyball, hiking, swimming, trampoline, stretching, working out, meditation, etc.
Social Cues	*Show up even as your child is seeming to be selfish or hard to get along with. She misses her friends' social cues that would normally tell her how to communicate in that group. She will compensate by either becoming angry to deflect her hurt or by withdrawing to pull away from it altogether.*

ISSUES	NEEDS
Social Cues (cont.)	Help your girl with social cues by spelling out your own reactions and feelings to interactions. When presented with problems, give your child options of possible different scenarios and examples of how she can react for greater success.
	Role playing can be very helpful and is a creative way to practice.
Talents and Skills	*Remember every girl on the spectrum has a secret skill or ability. Natural talents and skills are often very present amidst the deficits of Autism. Find ways to nurture these gifts to offset the challenges she will face.*
	Help her find it by really paying attention to what she CAN do and not so much what she can't do.
	Show her examples of people with a skill and/or talent she likes or is good at, and then teach her how that person took classes or learned more.
	Girls on the spectrum will often think that people are born that way and actually feel bad when their amazing talent isn't as good as professionals they encounter.
Theory of Mind Issues	*The inability to know what others are thinking and feeling will cause her to seem selfish and unreasonable when others are experiencing issues and her demands on them don't adjust.*
	"Theory of mind" prevents her from understanding what others are thinking and going through.
	Give her lots of opportunities to understand by sharing your own thoughts about things out loud (e.g., "I'm not talking to you right now because I have a headache and it hurts to talk. When I feel better, we can talk about how your day was.").
	Give her a possible idea of what friends may be thinking (e.g., "Maybe your friend is just tired today. You know how you don't feel like talking to people when you are tired?").

ISSUES	NEEDS
Valued and Appreciated	*Our girls desire to be valued and appreciated.* Need to know they are loved and important despite the difficult job they challenge you with. Write them notes that express how much they matter to you.
Verbal Expression vs. Monologues	*Girls on the spectrum learn to monologue but struggle to verbally express their authentic self.* Use alternative ways to communicate (e.g., a notepad, diary, assisted communication device). Remember to give them a script for this when they are overwhelmed (e.g., "Can I have my notepad?" etc.).

Final thoughts:

Scripts, scripts, and more scripts. Teach your girl how to get what she needs and wants with words that work. Once she masters that, show her how to say things differently with different people so she understands the depth of language.

Girls can often be very emotional and sensing individuals; add autism and you can have a super emotional and super sensing individual. The best way to interact with this type of soul is with honesty and love. You can't go too wrong if you approach all issues this way. Help your child feel supported by reminding her that you will figure out life together and that she is not alone. Consciously remain the person your child can turn to, so that in times of trouble she will always have an ally in you. If you make mistakes, and you will, apologize genuinely and talk about ways to do things differently next time. If things get heated or you see signs of distress, write or draw instead of speaking words. Like any parent or guardian of a girl, you will have your own feelings of frustration and defeat. Communicate them so she knows she is not alone with these experiences.

Love really is the great healer.

12 **Still Your Child**

Ondrea Marisa Robinson

In order to accept someone for who they are, you have to be aware of what's going on.

THERE ARE A LOT OF THINGS that I wish every parent of a child with autism knew, and I feel very strongly about that. Autism is not an easy developmental condition to deal with, especially if the parents do not really know how to deal with their kids, or if it is misinterpreted as something else. This is why there should be more autism awareness, as well as autism acceptance: because in order to accept someone for who they are, you have to be aware of what's going on.

Some of the things that I will explain, which parents need to know, are that their kids are children, are sensitive to noises, have a tough time communicating, have trouble with social interactions, and need to be loved unconditionally, no matter what. Kids diagnosed on the autism spectrum have it hard enough as it is!

Every parent has to remember that their kids with autism are children, and sometimes they might seem younger than their actual age. A parent should explain to their child about having autism in a way that the child can understand. One way is to explain that your child is different and that their brain processes differently from someone who does not have autism. Also, it is not anyone's fault, especially hers, that she has autism.

Being sensitive to noises is a big component of challenges for kids on the autism spectrum. When I was younger, I certainly did not like a lot of noises, because they were annoying, and my sensory processing was totally different. In fact, I would get scared, especially if there was a fire drill bell ringing at school. Sure, I went outside and didn't cause too much havoc by screaming, but it was still a pain even though fire drills had to be done. People with autism have sensory processing issues when it comes to different noises, but every person is different in how they process noise.

Just because children with autism have trouble communicating does not mean they cannot communicate. Sometimes when they get very upset, they don't know how to communicate properly, and they are misunderstood as being rude or being ignorant. They are just trying to get people's attention to get them to listen. I should know, because even though yelling may not be the best way to get someone's attention, sometimes it is pretty effective because it does get someone to listen, at least. Of course, there are calmer ways to communicate if parents show their children how to do it with patience and love.

Social interactions can be troublesome for a child on the autism spectrum. Sometimes your child may mean well, but some people may take things the wrong way. For example, just because your child is friendly to everyone does not mean that everyone will be nice to them. In fact, if your child says something that people may not understand, they might even laugh or call your child names, which does hurt! I should know, because I was that girl at one time, and believe me, it was not a pretty sight at times. I was picked on because social interactions were hard for me at one point. It's much better now with me in terms of social interactions, but I know I still have a lot of work to do.

All parents should love their kids with autism unconditionally, no matter what. Just because their kids are different in their own way does not mean the parents have to love them any less. At first, it may be hard for parents to accept the fact that their children have autism, and sometimes parents want a cure or even wish that autism never existed in the family, which is a sad reality. This is where autism acceptance comes in. Every parent will not be alike when it comes to autism acceptance, and other people do not have to like it, but they can respect it.

In conclusion, every parent of a child with autism should know as much as they need to know, especially when it comes to knowing what they can expect, especially when a child gets diagnosed. As I stated earlier, autism is not an easy developmental condition to deal with, but it is doable. People on the autism spectrum can live productive lives, just like everyone else. I should know, because I was one of those girls who lived a productive life with autism, and I am a young woman who is living a productive life with autism. I am thankful to have written this chapter.

13 Perfect in an Imperfect World

Haley Moss

It is not your or your child's job to set the world on fire, but to simply change perceptions one person at a time.

DEAR PARENTS,

Answering the question what I wished every parent of an autistic child knew is no easy feat, since there is no one correct answer.

I was once your child's age. I was diagnosed at age three and my parents once heard those fear-inducing words that I'm sure you've heard before: "Your child has autism." I'm sure you've heard them, too, which is why I'm going to try to answer your question as best I can and not lead you on that life on the spectrum is sunshine and roses all the time. Life has its ups and downs, regardless. I—like many other autistic women—face the realities, successes, and triumphs of being an autistic woman. And I face them every day with every breath I take in this world.

Your job as a parent to your child began before you knew your child was autistic. You signed up for this when, in your hearts, you knew you would be welcoming a child into your life, and you promised to love them forever. Even though I'm an adult, my parents are there for me every step of the way. Yes, they might have lightened up on their grip since I was a teenager or a fearful kid at a sleepover, but they are still there for me through and through. There are no others in this world that I would turn to as my best friends and biggest cheerleaders to confide in or who I know love me as unconditionally as my mom and dad. You are a parent before a friend, before anything else, and I beg of you to always be there for your child. They will love you, respect you, and see you as a role model. Be there for them. That is the easiest and simplest piece of advice I will give you today.

The next piece of advice I am going to give you is simple in theory and difficult in execution, since there is no timeline. But be comfortable in your child's autistic identity. Do not be afraid. Do not fear the rest of the world's reactions. Celebration and acceptance of diversity begins in your own home, with you.

Stand up for your child in any situation where people say negative things about autism, disability, or any other identities your family or child may have. It's okay to feel uncomfortable when people say the dreaded R-word, and to tell people you feel uncomfortable with it. It is something I do far more often than I would like to, but it's the first step you can take towards acceptance. When someone says something mean about autism, fight back gently: Tell them you're uncomfortable, that you'd prefer them to use different language. Keep the conversation on diversity open in your home and your life. As your child's parents and advocates, it should also show that you are comfortable with differences, so your child will be as well.

Know your child is not a victim, or a demon that you may have seen on television. Autism unfortunately has a bad rap, especially if you watch too much TV. You might have seen faces of murderers, of parents doing horrible things to autistic children, or of characters who embrace ingrained societal stereotypes about autism. Your child is more than a stereotype or a victim. They are a person just like you, and those around you are people. If you have an autistic daughter, she is not her male autistic counterpart, so you cannot generalize based on stereotypes either. She is an individual. You are also not the parent who would treat your kid as less than a person. You might be stressed, you might have your own issues with your parenting or in your marriage or at your place of employment, but your kid is not a victim of your life. I know you value your children, so please cherish them and their individuality!

■■■■■■

Do not be afraid to tell your daughter she is autistic. Sooner or later, she will figure out she is not like the others. She might realize she is not like her older sister, or her younger brother with all of his friends, or even a stranger who is the same age. Do not let her go through life wondering why or burden her with this information suddenly when she is eighteen years old and thus responsible for it as an adult. Only you will know when she is ready to understand her own identity, and that there is nothing to be ashamed of! I was ready at age nine. I figured there was something different about me, or different about everyone else. Thankfully, like most autistics, I had a special interest. At the time, it was Harry Potter, and that's how I found out. My mom likened having autism to having magic, kind of like how Harry was different from the Muggles (non-wizards and witches). In that sense, I learned that it is more than okay to be different than my peers. I am awesome. That's what I got out of how I found out, and we elaborated on the strengths of being autistic rather than the weaknesses. Autism was always viewed positively in our home. What kid wants to be reminded of their social deficits, picky eating, and other quirky (and often negatively portrayed) traits? We are more self-aware than you may give us credit for.

The way I found out about autism is not something I would change. I am proud that my parents waited until it seemed right, and made sense, and was applicable to my own nine-year-old self's world. Harry Potter was the perfect role model and an example of someone who is different from his peers but is still awesome. I would not change the way I looked at autism as a strength, but I wish I had been prepared for the way other people would look at me and exploit it as a weakness. Those are lessons that time has taught me.

I eventually learned that autism comes with imperfections and that the path is not all rainbows and butterflies. My weaknesses in picky eating, social deficits, etc., are a part of being on the autism spectrum.

An autism label also comes with some not-so-beautiful truths that none of us were prepared for. You will learn about the discrimination, stigmas, fear, and self-doubt that autistic people face. I want you to know that even though I tell you to champion your child, to be supportive and build their confidence, know that it may be torn down at some point by the outside world. In your eyes, and in mine, your child will be perfect in an imperfect world. The outside world might tell your child they are less because they are autistic. Some may assume incompetence because they know your child is autistic, but they do not know what your child is capable of. It is not yours or your child's job to set the world on fire and make everyone in this world accept them, and their fellow autistic people, for who they are, but to simply change perceptions one person at a time. I have been discriminated against and been told very hurtful things because I am autistic. I'm sure you can't even count how many times you've been told your child doesn't "look autistic," just like I can't. We look like every other child who smiles and enjoys the things that make us happy, and that, my friends, is what "looking autistic" is: looking like everyone else living life their own way!

I have no choice but to artfully fight back when someone assumes I am less of a person because of my identities as a woman and an autistic. In education, I have been told I would not get into college because I have a disability, and I have even been asked how I got into the University of Florida. My answer? The same way everyone else gets into college or the University of Florida: hard work, good grades, good essays—autism or not. Yes, it is sad that I must clarify that; however, the world doesn't always understand. I have been passed over for positions, jobs, and honors because a Google search (and my own mouth, if the situation calls for it) discloses that I am on the autism spectrum. Know that this will happen at some point in your child's life, whether it is at age eight or age eighteen. Be a good listener, console your child, and tell them it is not their fault. It is never, ever your child's—or any autistic person's—fault that they are autistic or treated differently than their peers. When your child is passed over, tell them to get back up and try again, and hopefully change someone's opinion. There are lessons and teachable moments in everything. My parents have always supported me, and it makes the blow of a hurtful comment so much easier to withstand.

Do not be afraid to ask questions about your child's life and inner self. The things that make up their world might be bigger to her than you may see. You might think a crush your child has is cute, but to them, it may mean the world. As I mentioned earlier, there may be a feeling of being uncomfortable in their autistic identity because of the discrimination, stigma, and anxiety that come with growing up, getting a real job, going to a good college, and making their way through life while facing the stigma that autism carries in our society.

Look for clues that something might be going on inside of your child's world, especially if you have an autistic daughter. Notice if she is anxious or upset or feeling not too great about herself. Look for whether she is withdrawn or seems overly moody. Do not blame it on hormones. It might be that she's having a bad day or that someone hurt her feelings. Do not trivialize the things in her life. You have no idea how big that thing might be in her life and may have no idea until it is too late or she feels she cannot trust you with it. I've had romantic partners, friends, and others write off autistic struggles as me being moody or hormonal or being too hard on myself. The fears I have about being an autistic adult or even a millennial are perfectly valid: How will the world treat me? Why is there such stigma and/or feelings of insecurity? (We all do at some point, whether it is in our identities or our bodies.) Do not be afraid to ask questions, since none of us are mind readers.

Do not be afraid to ask her what her life is like inside of autism. There are things parents, friends, professionals, and "outsiders" who don't live with autism in their lives do not understand or experience. Many people are like me and have sensory aversions. I was in the car with my mom the other day, on the way home from a frenzied sale in one of my favorite stores. It was overwhelming, so when we got to the car, I asked my mom to turn the radio down because I was drained from the shopping. "I never completely understood why the sensory thing overloads you. I mean, it was definitely hard to shop there when there were 150 girls in a small space, but I don't know what it's like for you," she said. I got to explain how my autistic brain fights the input of sensory stuff: pulsating electronic dance/pop music, crowds, disorganization, screaming girls, and warm air from tightly packed bodies in a store. My body fights it with its own output, and it is exhausting. I grow tired from trying to handle the sensory input from my environment; it might be a knot in my stomach, heavy breathing, or distracting my senses otherwise. Getting to explain this made more sense to an outsider than just having these feelings in a random moment.

Someday, she will ask you questions, too, and those questions will keep you awake at night. It might be something like "Am I pretty?" or "Am I worth it?" or "Can you help me?" or "Why am I so different from everyone else?" The "difference" conversation is a hard one, and I know that when I got older, knowing I was autistic was a blessing and a curse. You think it is great because of the talents and gifts that make you unique but see it differently when you feel isolated and are struggling with your peers, especially when you compare what they are doing and what you are doing and they don't line up. It is your job to be your daughter's champion in a world where autism is still stigmatized and where women everywhere are expected to be an ideal she may feel she doesn't meet. Let her know she is beautiful inside and out. Let her know the world is a better place because she is in it, and all her unique challenges and abilities make her the little lady she is. As far as comparing myself to my peers, I will tell you that I'm guilty. I wonder why I don't have friends who text me every five seconds, plans every Friday night, and a constant need to drive my car like most other young women my age. It took me a long time to be comfortable knowing that I am not like everybody else and that what I see on Facebook isn't the truth: people only show what they want you to see. It is okay not to be living the way everyone else is, and neurotypical people, who seem to have happy, perfect lives, surprise me when they say they aren't happy. I have friends who live the way I envied because it seems social, but it turns out not everything is how it appears. They are lonely, they have hopes and dreams and fears, and they are human, just like me, just like you, and just like your child.

Support her interests as well, no matter what your personal opinion of them is. She might be insecure about her hobbies and interests as she gets older if they are not "age appropriate" or "girly" or whatever societal label is placed upon the things your autistic daughter loves most. Learn to participate in her interests and ask lots of questions, even if it bores you to tears to hear about Harry Potter for the millionth time. She will appreciate the fact that you want to listen and care, and you will admire the passion she has when speaking about her interest in the wizarding world. Autism has given me a range of interests and likes from video games, to Hello Kitty, to all things creative.

Let me tell you a story about having "gender-inappropriate" and "age-appropriate" interests. Growing up, I loved playing video games and trading cards (Yu-Gi-Oh!, in particular). In grade school, I made friends with all the boys because we played games together and traded cards. At the time, I had no friends who were girls because girls didn't play video games. Girls in the fourth grade didn't care about Yu-Gi-Oh! cards, but they cared about horses, Bratz and Barbie dolls, pop music they were too young to understand, and their growing curiosity about shopping and makeup. At one point, it was suggested that I get friendlier with the girls to understand their interests and abandon the boys, but I, fourth-grader Haley, wasn't hearing it. I am in my twenties and still enjoy a good video game, even if the target audience is "age 7 and older" on the box. I was embarrassed when I bought a new handheld console and Pokémon game because I thought I was "too old," since most of the boys had moved on to shooter games, Steam, PlayStation 4, or Xbox, and young adult women don't play video games of any kind. I knew it was something my friends would laugh at me for, so my special interest from my youth became something I'd do late at night when friends and family weren't around or sleeping. It stung, feeling like I had to be ashamed of something I loved so much because of society's expectations, and I couldn't talk about it with anyone I knew in the real world; I had to get my fix reading and playing online. One day, my mom wanted to check out my new handheld system and said how cool the graphics were. Video games were never her thing. I swear, she only knew because I was too excited to keep playing and couldn't wait until I had "alone time." That day, I looked at her with embarrassment at getting caught, and with sheepish shame in my voice, I asked: "Am I too old for this? I bought the system when I was at college so you and Daddy wouldn't judge me." She gave the answer I wanted to hear when I unwillingly traded my Yu-Gi-Oh! cards for Bratz dolls in the fourth grade: "Of course not, as long as it makes you happy."

Had I heard "as long as it makes you happy" in fourth grade the way I did last summer, maybe I would've kept doing my thing and had the confidence to keep playing in middle school. Instead, I felt I had to give up my interests to blend in, like when I traded my rare cards for Bratz dolls. I learned that it's okay to like everything I like and dislike what society tells me to like: I love to shop (that took a lot of years to happen, so don't freak out if your autistic daughter hates shopping at a young age), I love video games (specifically those with Nintendo or Sega characters), I love my artist markers, I dislike makeup as a hobby (it's confusing, and shopping for it is hard), I dislike taking selfies, and I dislike sports.

One day, the things your daughter likes and has interests in may become more than that. They will turn into aspirations, goals, careers, and more. Support her dreams every step of the way. I am sure that as a parent you want the best for her and want her to be happy, and if you support the dreams she wants to chase, it will be worthwhile. Do not make her dreams about the money, the stability, etc. If she won't stop drawing, encourage her to continue and maybe she will be an artist. If she shares her dreams with you, don't

Artist Haley Moss wants her artwork, What Every Autistic Girl Wishes Her Parents Knew, *to reflect both the hopes of autistic girls for acceptance and support from our families and the dreams of parents for their autistic daughters.*

be afraid to help her pursue them. Do not push her into a career, a college, or anything she does not want to do. As a parent you know what is best for her, but don't be afraid to let her spread her wings and fly. I knew living away from home would be hard. Sure, my parents would've been proud for me to go to an Ivy League school, but I knew I couldn't handle the pressure and being that far away from home. I did not feel like I disappointed or let anyone down by going to school in-state so that I could come home, and I chased after what I wanted: to keep advocating for the autism community, artwork, and even a bit of law to help protect my wonderful disability and autism communities. It is all about supporting interests and dreams, because without the support of my family, I would not be where I am today.

Dear parents, I am sorry if this letter comes off as an elementary course in how to accept your autistic child for who they are. However, you understanding your child and having open conversations and pride in everything they are and do is so important, and it is the difference between an angry child who wishes they were neurotypical and a child who delights in the quirkiness and beauty of their autistic self. I hope you have the type of child who will live their life fearlessly, unafraid of the world ahead, and brave enough to use their words or experiences to show that autism is not something to be ashamed of, embarrassed about, or an inner demon. And to raise a child like that—one who is so confident in their own skin—begins with you. I believe in you, as a parent, and I wish you and your child the best, and I hope one day they join the proud autistic community alongside me and countless others.

Thank you so much for listening, and I hope one day I am as courageous as you to ask for unbiased, realistic advice and help when I feel I need it.

Your new autistic friend,
Haley Moss

14 Who Gets to Be Diagnosed? And Who Does It Serve?

Victoria M. Rodríguez-Roldán

Nobody is worthless; nobody should face lessened prospects or mistreatment because of who they are.

▬▬▬

ONE OF THE PERENNIAL DEBATES in the autistic community is the topic of self-diagnosis. As someone who only "came out" as autistic in her adulthood, that is rather personal to me. Many people often try to invalidate the experience of autistic people who either realized their disability as adults or simply were never diagnosed by a clinician.

In my case, I learned as an adult that my mother had been encouraged to get me "tested" for autism, but she had refused. And it tracks with the type of mother she was. She needed to see me as perfect and destined for greatness, and my being a near-gifted child with many academic honors only reinforced the idea that there was no way I could have intellectual or mental health disabilities. If she and the other adult figures in my life had a mental image or stereotype of what an autistic child looked like, it was the "low-functioning" (use of quotation marks intentional) child who is non-oral and is regarded as the R-word.

In some ways, I wish my mother had followed that advice and prospect with an open mind and taken the steps to get me a diagnosis. Maybe it would have been validating for me in adulthood to have had that. Maybe I would have received accommodations at some point that might have made my school years a bit less miserable. Who knows?

The truly big conclusion I've come to is that it was probably for the best that I never got diagnosed and flew under the radar.

And the reason for that goes beyond the fact that it was the 1990s, though that forms part of it.

To get there, we have to answer a couple questions: First, who gets to have a childhood diagnosis? Second, what effect does it have? So, who gets to have a diagnosis in the first place? Well, we can discuss privilege, to begin with. If you have good insurance and access to genuinely nonjudgmental psych specialists, you might be in luck. That already is leaving out a lot of the population. People with low income or limited access to healthcare have a lower likelihood of getting in through that front door. We must also take into account that people of color and women are less likely to have their concerns taken seriously by healthcare professionals. So, the people with the most access to a diagnosis are going to be primarily white, affluent, and well insured.

That is the obvious part. But, also, what impact does the diagnosis have? Often, among us disabled and chronically ill people, getting a diagnosis is a joyous moment, since it comes with answers and explanations as to whatever trials and tribulations we might have been experiencing to date. But outside our community, abled people often treat a major diagnosis as some tragedy that requires a mournful violin soundtrack. Autistic youth are routinely shunted into tortures like ABA therapy and segregated schooling, and unless the parents know better and fight for their kid, they are frequently sold the story by educators and therapists that their kid will "never amount to much," so to speak. Throw in all the stereotypes often perpetuated by providers themselves (lacking in empathy, low emotional intelligence, will never find love, etc.)—I can keep on going. There's a reason that as neurodiverse people, almost none of us wants to relive our childhoods. This one is part of that reason.

And thus, I wonder: How would I have been treated by the adults in my life had I gotten that diagnosis back then? Would I have gotten the amazing help I needed, or would I have been shunted into abusive "therapies" that would only have made my childhood even worse than it actually was? Would my parents have still put the effort and expense into channeling me to good schools, with higher education and a professional career already a foregone conclusion? Would the "extreme male brain" stereotype have been used as one more weapon against me when I came out as trans later in the early to mid-2000s?

Sadly, given the time and place and realities in question, I have to admit that it was probably for the best that I never got the vaunted diagnosis to begin with. In a weird way, it is its own privilege—that one of my disabilities flew under the radar and wasn't used as a weapon against me.

But that speaks volumes and is in some ways what every parent should know: Your child does not have to be perfect, and your child isn't a failure because they are or may be autistic. And you should allow no one to tell you that they'll amount to less or are worth less, or that they should receive subpar treatment. Give them the best. Nobody is worthless; nobody should face lessened prospects or mistreatment because of who they are. Your role is to ensure that for your children.

15 Unconventional

Amythest Schaber

Normality is not a virtue, and defiance of the norm is not a sin.

I HAVE A GOOD LIFE. It did not come easily. It is a labor of love, built out of improvised material and held together by hard work. I have a good life because of the care and effort of myself, my partner, and my chosen family and friends.

I am a Métis, chronically ill, multiply disabled, nonbinary autistic person. I grew up poor, and my home life was tumultuous and emotionally unsafe. My childhood was defined by instability and profound loneliness. Against the odds, I have a good life now. But if you look at it from the outside, you might not see it the way I do. If you value convention, you may even disagree.

Where I grew up, convention decrees that you are either a boy or a girl. That you are white—the perceived default—or not. That you are either disabled or gifted, impaired all the time or never impaired. That your relationships will fall into defined categories and follow an expected trajectory. That you will eventually assimilate into a monolithic adulthood, grow up into a standard mold.

I think of the word "adulthood" and picture rows of square watermelons, but you may disagree. The things that feel so restrictive and ill-fitting to me may be familiar and comforting to you.

Differences can be a profound source of discomfort between people. When the person in question is your own child, that discomfort can hurt your child. If loving effort is not made to accept what is different, those differences become chasms, and disapproval of someone's true self burns bridges faster than we can build them.

Children are their own people and will grow up to want and not want things for themselves that their parents didn't expect. When it comes to autistic children of non-autistic parents, this is especially true. As a parent you likely have a dream for your child's life, a wish list of all the good things you expect for them. You have to be careful with expectations.

Some autistic people will never live unassisted. Many will never have a traditional career or meet abled standards of productivity under capitalism. These things do not preclude a good life. Overwhelmingly, what parents who reach out to me want for their children is for them to be happy. There are some who are fixated on normality, who are hung up on non-autistic, non-disabled measurements of adulthood and success. But mostly, people just want to know how to help their children grow up into happy, healthy autistic people.

When you let go of expectations, your hands are free to embrace your child for who they are. When you prioritize happiness over convention, you can focus on helping them make a life that suits them well.

Which brings us to what I most want parents of autistic children to understand: You don't have to understand someone to love them. You don't have to agree on what brings joy or defines success to accept them and celebrate their happiness with them.

Having a parent who values and expects adherence to non-disabled, non-autistic convention is deeply harmful for autistic children. A parent's role is to provide unconditional love and support for their child. Everyone deserves to know that they are not only accepted for who they are but that they are valued.

There is an undeniable link between being autistic and being transgender. It is not yet understood, but more and more autistic people are sharing their experiences as this topic gains traction in the community. Many autistic people identify as gender non-conforming or other nonbinary identities, or as having a unique relationship to gender that is informed by their neurotype and makes it impossible to tease apart from being autistic.

It's another difficult thing to quantify, but autistic people may also be more likely to identify as gay, lesbian, bisexual, asexual, queer, and other orientations other than straight. Is it that autistic people are more likely to be trans and to have marginalized sexual identities? Or that we are more likely to defy societal norms and openly identify as such? No one can say yet, but regardless of the how or why, there is a link there.

Being anything but cisgender and straight is not the norm, but neither is it wrong. This is also true of disability. Being autistic is not the norm, but it isn't wrong. The lives that autistic people build for themselves may not be conventional, but they aren't inferior.

Every person will form relationships during their lifetime, and relationships often look different for autistic people. Some autistic people do date, eventually marry, choose to have children, or some combination of those three things. Some autistic people do make families that would be classified as conventional, as "normal," but some do not. I know many autistic people who have made unconventional families for themselves.

Unconventional families can look like living with good friends or being a part of a communal living situation. It can look like living with family members whose values align with your own or choosing your own family. There are autistic people, like me, who have platonic life partners, who have committed to making a life together with a dear and trusted friend. Sometimes our friends and partners are also our caregivers.

Are those choices typical or conventional? No, but convention does not promise happiness, and in the case of people whose lived experiences and whose needs are so fundamentally different from the norm, trying to force what is typical is hurtful.

If you are autistic and grow up hearing that your parent had hoped for a typical, non-autistic child—that who you are is a disappointment, a mistake, a loss—that wounds deeply. As has been said over and over, by autistic people who have been advocating and educating for much longer than I have, there is no hating the autism and loving the child. Making an autistic person conform to non-autistic ideals, by force or coercion, is cruelty. And even if you choose acceptance and love, the world will put pressure on your autistic child, and no society is free of the ableist messages that lead to self-loathing, anxiety, and depression.

But you can combat these messages with these truths: normality is not a virtue, and defiance of the norm is not a sin. Just because something is typical does not mean it's the best way to be. With acceptance and support, disabled people can and do lead happy, fulfilling lives—our lives are just very rarely conventional.

But to choose what makes you happy, you have to know that it is an option. Much of this discovery happens through the trial and error of growing up, but you can start with a strong base. I encourage the parents of autistic children to do two things: develop relationships with adult autistic people when you can and consistently affirm that there are many ways of being.

By modeling respect for all kinds of people and by demonstrating acceptance for all kinds of lives that people live, you are also instilling self-love and building a foundation on which your child can picture their own happiness. By having autistic friends and by letting your child know and learn from autistic adults, you can combat the ableist messages we all grow up hearing.

As a child I had a remarkable imagination, but I couldn't picture my own adulthood. I dreaded the things that I had been told were mandatory and must be done in the typical way: living on my own, making a career, getting married, having children. I feared having to comply and be unhappy. Knowing an autistic adult who prioritized their happiness over typicality would have meant the world to me.

Now, I have a good life. It's not without difficulties, but there is so much to be thankful for. If I could, I would take my own hand and tell my younger self that there is nothing wrong with them. That they don't need to comply with societal norms to be happy. That they will be accepted and loved, and that they will have wonderful friendships that don't look anything like non-autistic friendships. I would tell them that abnormality can fit like a dream, if you have the courage to try it on.

For me, those years of struggle and pain will have to remain. But you have opportunity at your fingertips, access to the hard-learned lessons of autistic adults who have been where your child is now. You can choose to apply this wisdom and give your child their best chance at happiness.

You can love your child unconditionally. You can accept them for who they are and, as they grow into autistic adulthood, respect the shape that their life takes. You can support their dreams, even if those dreams are nothing like what you would choose, and keep an open mind as you do. It may be hard work, but I promise you this: there is joy and wonder to be found in the unconventional.

16 I Wish I Wasn't So Hard on Myself Back Then

Kayla Smith

I want to tell the younger generation, "You were born right the first time, and don't be ashamed of it."

THE JOURNEY OF MY LIFE has been filled with joy, laughter, and excitement, as well as sadness, worry, and disappointment. In many ways, it may seem that I have a "normal" life just like everybody else, but I know that I don't. Whether I want to admit it or not, I often feel like I am in my own little world and that I don't belong anywhere. I always feel out of place and don't know why I feel the way that I do. I live in a world that doesn't see me as a human being because I am a Black autistic woman. I don't understand why the world dislikes me and wants me to assimilate to the standards of what a person "should" be like instead of letting me and others who are different be ourselves at all.

Until recently, I hadn't spent much time reflecting upon the past, but lately I've been thinking a lot about my younger years up to recent days. As I look back at my life, I feel that I had a nice childhood. I liked spending the night at my cousin's house, having cookouts with my family, and going to school. I can't really remember everything from that time but for the most part, I was just living life as a kid and all. I do have a supportive family. They love and adore me. At the same time, and even now, my family sometimes doesn't get me or understand me, and I find myself getting very frustrated.

When I was growing up, over time I started noticing some things that made me realize that I was different from other kids: Like how I would go to speech therapy (I was nonverbal until I was six years old). How people would say, "Pray for Kayla," like something was wrong with me. And how I had people teach me life skills like how to count money, how to eat, etc. Also, in elementary school I was in special education classes. I had regular classes, too, because I have always loved learning no matter what the subject was—science, math, history, English (my favorite subject is math). I was also tomboyish. I felt more comfortable with boys than with girls because in a lot of my classes I was the only girl.

I had a hard time having social conversation. Sometimes I didn't understand what people were saying and I got overwhelmed and confused. I would go to another room where no one was there and stay there until I got my energy back. I found out that I didn't like some noises because they hurt my ears and that I could not focus with all the noise around me. Sometimes I got bullied by other kids. I didn't know why those kids were bullying me and looking at me funny. Being as young as I was, I may or may not have paid attention to them then. I was mostly just minding my own business.

The first things I learned about autism came from my family. I was diagnosed with autism when I was two years old, and I found out that I was autistic when I was ten years old from my mom, who told me, "Autism is what you have, and it does not define you." I had a neutral reaction when I learned about my diagnosis. As I got older, I started to research my diagnosis and tried to understand more about it. Being as curious as I am, I would go to websites and look up "autism" and "girls" and "autistic girls." I found a lot of information about autistic girls, and I could relate to most of what it is like to be an autistic girl. I found out that girls who are autistic are more likely to be misdiagnosed than boys. I found it very interesting. But when I looked up "Black autistic girls," hoping to find out more about people who looked like me, I didn't see any information about this. At the time I did not ask myself why, but I found out later that it is because of a lack of representation of autistic people of color.

Once I knew about my diagnosis, I didn't mind telling people that I am autistic. But all people would do is say, "Okay," or "I don't know anything about autism at all." I started getting bullied more, quite a bit, and I kinda started to hate myself for being different. I remember asking myself "Why me?" and wishing I didn't have it. I became ashamed of myself. Then I remembered what my mom said when I was ten years old: "Don't let autism define you." So, as a teenager, I got hard on myself and tried to be perfect at everything. I developed a mentality that I could "beat" autism and that I was an autism warrior (it wasn't until later I found out that is offensive and filled with internalized ableism).

I tried to fit in. I spent most of my life trying to "prove" to people that I didn't let autism "define me" and that I could do the same things as everybody else. I struggled with my identity and how I saw myself in the world. For years, I tried to be somebody that I was not, and I was not happy. I felt like I was living a lie every day of my life. Sadly, in my teenage years, I was so unhappy that I thought about committing suicide, but I never had the guts to do it, so I did not try to commit suicide even though deep inside I wanted to.

I even lost my Supplemental Security Income (SSI) and Medicaid because I was so focused on trying to prove to everyone that I don't let autism "define me," even though I do have medical needs. Recently, I tried to apply to get Medicaid back and SSI. I called the Social Security office to find out how to get it back. The person asked me how "severely disabled" I was, and I was thinking to myself, "Why do I have to prove to you how severely disabled I am to get my SSI back? Are you kidding me?" I was so upset, and I said forget it. First the world says not to let autism "define you." Now, all of sudden, when I need help, I have to prove to people that I am autistic.

Now, I regret all those years that I didn't accept who I am. I wish that I never did that to myself, and I feel like crap thinking about it now, and I am trying to unlearn my internalized ableism little by little and be comfortable in my own skin as an autistic person. Now, I wonder why I did this to myself growing up. I realize I am living in an ableist society that discriminates against me because I am autistic. The ableist society doesn't see autistic people or disabled people as human beings but instead sees people like me as a tragedy. The ableist society uses the medical model of disability against disabled people to convince us that it is better to be normal than being disabled or autistic. Not only do I have to deal with systemic ableism; I must deal with systemic racism and sexism as well. I was like, "Damn, I have to deal with never-ending bullshit for the rest of my life." I am a triple threat (Black, autistic, and a woman), and intersectionality can be very complicated. It looks like I have to fight for my rights and respect in a racist, sexist, and ableist society.

To make things even sadder, I have been through all of this and I am only in my twenties. I know I have more life to live and a long way to go, but I still don't know who I am and what my purpose is. For me, I am the kind of person who likes to figure things out and go with it. I realize now that's not always as simple as it seems. For now, I am living life day by day. Maybe I need to focus on myself more and figure out what I, Kayla, want out of life without someone telling her how to live it. As I got older, I realized I had more to learn. Hopefully, I can find something that I need to work on and what I need to let go of.

The reason I am telling my story is because other disabled people around the world may have a similar experience as me. I know I can't speak for all disabled or autistic people around the world, but I hope I can share my story and reach people who can relate to me on certain issues. I don't want young autistic or disabled children to feel the same way I did. I don't want this hurt and rejection to repeat itself in the next generation and to have future generations feel like we are a tragedy and that it is better to be "normal." I want to tell the younger generation that you are born right the first time and to not be ashamed of it. Yes, you have good and bad times that come with being disabled, and that's okay. I want the neurotypical, abled people to be better allies to the disability community and unlearn ableist bias, ensuring buildings, events, and things are accessible and inclusive to disabled people—and hopefully end ableism for good. It will take a while to get there, but I hope to one day live in a world where I am not judged on the basis of my disability. Education is needed, and it needs to start now. Let's fight for acceptance for disabled people.

17 Ten Things I Wish
My Parents Had Known
When I Was Growing Up

Amelia "Mel" Evelyn Voicy Baggs

You can't put a price tag on freedom.

I'VE BEEN ASKED to write something from the perspective of a "high needs" autistic person. By which they seem to mean someone who needs a lot of services in order to survive. Which is a category I do fall into. I wish I could have written something a lot more thorough and in-depth, but in the middle of the time I should have been writing, I moved into a new apartment and my father died of cancer. I hope that will explain why this isn't the best or most thorough writing I've ever done in my life. So, here are some things you should know about having a daughter growing into adulthood with "high needs" autism.

My name is Mel Baggs, short for Amelia Evelyn Voicy Baggs. I am a crocheter, a poet, a painter, a writer, a self-advocate, and an autistic person. I have multiple disabilities that can't easily be teased apart from each other. Many of them run in my family. My family doesn't really have non-disabled people in it, so I had the luck to grow up thinking that at least some degree of disability is normal. In the past I've needed a wheelchair to get around, but right now I can make it with a cane or crutches—sometimes without either. I was bedridden for six years with a combination of severe adrenal insufficiency and myasthenia gravis (or possibly hereditary myasthenia, but that's splitting hairs). I use a keyboard to communicate. I have a lot of different assistive technology.

I was diagnosed with PDD-NOS (pervasive developmental disorder-not otherwise specified)/atypical autism at the age of fourteen; at least that's what it said on paper. My doctor used the words "idiot savant" and "autistic." But back in the 1990s, "autistic" could mean a life sentence to an institution, and he wanted to avoid that, so he used the mildest category he could get away with. We still had to fight to keep me out of permanent institutional placement, regardless. Sometime around 1999, my diagnosis was changed back to just plain autistic disorder, and in 2000, my diagnosis was changed to autistic disorder with catatonia. Not because I'd changed, but because it was no longer dangerous to have a diagnosis of autistic disorder and because my shrink had finally (thanks to a self-advocacy group I was part of) gotten hold of the paper "Catatonia in Autistic Spectrum Disorders," by Lorna Wing and Amitta Shah.[1]

I live in my own apartment and am about to get a roommate because it's getting harder to do things again. I have a good deal of services with people helping me out with every aspect of daily living. It doesn't sound like much, especially when you know I'm unemployed. But when I was a teenager, I was planning out how to live in the woods as a hermit, to avoid permanent institutionalization. And when I realized that wouldn't work, I was planning my own death. It was only after I was exposed to severely disabled developmentally disabled adults (autistic and non-autistic) that I was able to envision a future for myself. Now I am about as happy and well-adjusted as someone from my background can get, I think. I am happier and more well-adjusted than a lot of people who are more "independent" than I am. Nobody is independent. Everyone is interdependent on each other. That's important to teach your kids, too. It's important, in general, to teach them that there are all kinds of futures, that people can live without jobs, without being able to take care of themselves, and without having to be institutionalized (including in group homes). It is also important to know the following:

1. *You may not always know she is high needs until she is put into a situation in which she can't function.*
In early childhood, I did lose my speech, but after a short delay, I regained something that looked like speech. I did reasonably well academically in elementary school, and I was generally on

the honor roll. I both skipped grades and was held back grades at different times. I even went to a year of college when I was fourteen. I was mainstreamed up until I was diagnosed at age fourteen, and after that I either didn't go to school, went to school in mental institutions, or went to school in special education programs that catered to people with a mix of psychiatric and developmental conditions. Then I went on to community college, where I did well for a year (which is more than I can say for my other attempt at college—I really *felt* good this time) but burned out again, and when I transferred to university, I couldn't even make it to class.

I moved out on my own at the age of nineteen, where I discovered that despite being trained in daily living skills at a residential facility *and* mental institution, I pretty much could not implement any of these skills. It's one thing to know in theory how skills work. It's another thing to put them into practice with nobody guiding you or prompting you along the way.

Worse, I was losing skills, including speech, at an alarming rate. The more skills I had to manage on my own, the less energy I had to put into other skills, and the more behind I got. This had been going on since early adolescence, but it really picked up the pace when I moved out on my own.

2. *Daily Living Skills training will not always work.*
It only works if the autistic person in question has the skills and the cognitive and physical stamina to implement the training. A person can seem to do really well in training in a controlled setting but do terribly in real life, and vice versa. I was closer to the first sort.

3. *A person who is unable to take care of themself does not have to live in any kind of institution, whether that be a group home, a large institution, or what I call "community institutionalization," where all the features of an institution still exist, but instead of walking from building to building, the person is driven from program to program.*

When I first moved out on my own, things were not looking good at all. I could do maybe one and a half daily living skills per day, on a good day, and most days weren't good days. I could not clean up after myself. I urinated on the living room floor and in the front yard. I banged my head on the wall or with my fists for a large portion of the day. I couldn't cook without starting fires, and I couldn't reliably remember to eat. I couldn't even remember there was food in the cupboards because I couldn't perceive it directly through my senses, so it didn't exist.

4. *Some autistic people suddenly gain skills in adolescence, some people suddenly lose skills, and some do both. In people who do both, one will generally be noticed over the other, which can be harmful.*

I've done a lot of digging through outcome studies to understand what happened to me. How I went from a verbal student on the honor roll to a special education student with only sporadic speech to a nonverbal adult who needs help with everything. And what I found surprised me.

It seems that between one-third and one-sixth of autistic people lose major skills in adolescence. Of those, about half will gain their skills back eventually and half won't. All autistic people show traits of catatonia, but only some autistic people will show traits of what is now called autistic catatonia, a movement disorder (not a psychiatric disorder) in which autistic people develop an increase in catatonic traits, have periods of slower movement, loss of speech, and an increased dependence on external prompts in order to get things done. You can read more about it in Wing and Shah's paper, "Catatonia in Autistic Spectrum Disorders."

While there is one "expert" out there who rather aggressively recommends electroconvulsive therapy (ECT) for severe autistic catatonia, all the autistic people I know who have autistic catatonia and got electroshock either got worse or stayed the same. One of them almost died, and it took years for her to get her life and memory back again. One particular researcher who recommends

ECT seems to be on a crusade to bring back ECT and normalize it again, because he only seems to research conditions for which ECT is traditionally used (severe catatonia, severe depression, etc.). He was not receptive to feedback from those of us who actually had autistic catatonia; in fact, he was rude to us and made a lot of unwarranted assumptions about the severity of the catatonia. (One woman he argued with had been immobilized for months at a time, and he told her she just didn't understand how bad it could be because some people froze for months at a time.)

Any kind of autistic person can get autistic catatonia. Whether they're labeled Asperger's, HFA (high-functioning autism), LFA (low-functioning autism), MFA (medium-functioning autism), autistic, PDD-NOS, or whatever. The only people who seem significantly more susceptible to autistic catatonia are people whose main social-relating style is social passivity. That means we will usually socialize when approached by others but that we can't easily approach others ourselves. I was very socially passive as a child, and I ended up with autistic catatonia starting at puberty.

5. *The more help we get, the more capable we are.*
Many parents are made to fear that if they give their autistic children help, then we will get lazy and never learn to do anything for ourselves. While I'm sure that happens sometimes, it's not usually the case.

Autistic author and artist Donna Williams often made the analogy of the straw that broke the camel's back. Giving autistic people help in order to function better, by giving us services that allow us to live on our own if we wish, takes straws off our backs. The more straws you remove from our backs, the more capable we become. This is the exact opposite of what you'd expect if we were really as lazy as some people assume we are.

When I was first living on my own, the only help I got was physical prompting from my cat and verbal prompting from a woman I met through a self-advocacy group, over the phone. I spent most of my day totally unable to control my body. Either I was immobilized and couldn't get started moving, or I was moving all over the place and couldn't stop moving. The prompting saved my life, but I was still starving and living in a filthy environment.

Today, I get three shifts of services throughout the day and an overnight shift when I can press a button and have someone here in less than five minutes. I get some kind of assistance with every daily living skill you can imagine. This ranges from total assistance to physical prompting to get started (for instance, I would never brush my teeth on my own, but if someone hands me a toothbrush, I can do it just fine most of the time). Because of the extensive assistance I get, I am able to put in time to write, to crochet, to help other people, and to do all kinds of things I could not do when I was trying to do everything by myself.

6. *There is no need, ever, for institutions. Don't put your child in one.*

Whatever you call them—ICF/MR (intermediate care facility for mental retardation, now known as intermediate care facilities for individuals with intellectual disabilities), ICF/DD (intermediate care facility for persons with developmental disabilities), group homes, residential facilities, private mental institutions, developmental centers, state psychiatric hospitals, or nursing homes— they're all institutions, and they all have the same soul-crushing aspects to them. So do the "community institutions" I mentioned earlier, as well as what have been called "pseudo-utopian farm communities," where parents build what they believe to be utopian group homes on farmland for their own children to live in for the rest of their lives.

There is nothing that can be done in an institution that can't be done—and done better—in someone's home. If there are no programs where you live for autistic people of *all* ability levels to live in our own homes (our own homes, not our parents' homes, unless that's really truly what we want) and get whatever assistance we need to do that, then you need to get busy making such things exist now, while your child is still young. I would not be living in my own apartment if Vermont self-advocates and parent-advocates hadn't spent decades lobbying for community-based services, something I'm incredibly grateful for. I've gone to the legislature myself to tell them my story and urge them not to cut these services. I've had people from the state say, "Her services are so expensive, why is she being allowed to live on her own?" Those are dangerous words. You can't put a price tag on freedom.

If you're interested in this, in the United States, I would look into the Community Imperative[2] (a declaration from Syracuse University supporting the rights of all disabled people to community living), all the different self-advocacy groups for people with developmental disabilities, ADAPT,[3] and anyone else who seems to be making an effort to change things for disabled people in this country.

Unfortunately, I don't have a lot of information on how other countries have done things. I just know that no matter where you are, institutions always do grave harm to those who live there, whether they can feel the harm happening at the time or not. Sometimes they're the best of a bunch of terrible options, but they're never good.

7. *Think about what's important.*
There are a lot of things I am not likely to ever learn how to do. Or if I learn how to do them, my movement disorders will prevent me from applying that knowledge. So, if I'm going to put in the extreme effort it takes for me to learn and sustain a skill, it had better be a skill that makes me happier (like crocheting), not just a skill that makes things easier on everyone else (like making my bed).

8. *Don't offer "hope" that is impossible. It can backfire considerably.*
Throughout my adolescence, there was an argument going on between the people who were treating me.

Some of them saw themselves as on the side of hope. They said that by my early twenties, if I wasn't cured, I would at least be close enough to normal to move out on my own into the mountains and write books and be a local eccentric.

Others saw themselves as "realists." They said that I would never get better and that, as a consequence, I would spend the rest of my life in an institution.

At first, it sounds like they're saying two very different things. But they're not. They're both saying, "If you don't get better, you'll be in an institution for the rest of your life." I knew I'd never get better, because I knew that every step forward was accompanied by five steps back, even when I was running as fast as I could to keep up with my same-age peers. I knew this in my bones. So, both sides were saying that this meant an institution for the rest of my life. This contributed to severe depression and suicide attempts. For years.

Nobody offered me what I got from the autistic community, which is the next point I'm going to make.

9. *Expose your child, early and often, to adults like themselves,*
   living good lives.
By "adults like themselves," I don't necessarily just mean autistic adults. I mean people who can't do the same things they can't do. I mean other people they can relate to, which even among the autistic spectrum is likely to be a minority. I would say that as cautiously as you can (because not all autistic adults are safe—there are child molesters and stalkers out there who are autistic and who target autistic kids), expose your children to the widest range of adults with developmental disabilities as you possibly can. And, specifically, expose your children to adults who are as severely disabled as they are, or even more severely disabled, but who live in their own apartments, even own their own houses, direct their own services to the best of their abilities, and take part in their communities. Show your child that they have a future whether they gain skills, lose skills, or stay the same. This is vital for suicide prevention.

We have to know. Literally have to, have to know. That we will be okay no matter what skills we learn, what skills we lose, and what skills we end up with by the time we grow up. That the world will have a place for us. That this place may not end up meaning living with you (for some of us, even with good parents, that's our worst nightmare). But that you will help us find a place for ourselves, whatever it takes, and no matter what our skills look like by adulthood.

10. *Do away with words like high- and low-functioning to describe your child.*

We hear you when you say things like that about us. We hear you when you call us retarded in front of other people, or even say we *look* retarded. We hear everything you say. And even if we don't immediately understand it, we may understand the gist of it from the tone, and through delayed language processing we may understand it days, months, years, or even decades later. Never assume we don't understand.

Also, don't compare us to other disabled people. Don't say things like, "You'll never need the kind of help Jerry gets; he has an IQ of 30 and yours is 130." Or "You'll never get the kind of opportunities Jerry gets; he has an IQ of 130 and yours is only 30." Don't use other disabled people in power plays to convince us to do what you want. Don't divide us into the good, obedient autistic people and the bad, disobedient autistic people (it's always the strongest self-advocates who get put in the second category).

Just don't compare. We already know there are vast differences between different kinds of autistic people. We already know that the differences that exist aren't the difference between autism and Asperger's, or HFA and LFA, but differences that have no names. Don't reinforce the idea that the autism "experts" have all the answers about who we are and what help we need. Don't fall into the trap of believing that if we are good at one thing, we will be good at some totally unrelated thing. Don't make it sound like any autistic person has a certain level of skills across the board. Autistic people's skills have been consistently described since the 1940s as being very uneven. There's a reason for that.

18 I Am an Autistic Woman

Amy Sequenzia

My world was ever expanding, but I was being pulled back from it.

I WRITE THIS not only from the point of view of an Autistic woman. What I have to say is about Autistic girls, Autistic boys, Autistic women, and Autistic men. It is about how important it is to understand our way of interacting with the world, how important it is that we rely on each other, and how important it is that neurotypical parents rely on us to help the younger and future generations of Autistics.

When I was about two years old, my diagnosis was PDD-NOS, although I think at the time it was simply PDD, or pervasive developmental disorder. Soon after, I was diagnosed as Autistic. Before the PDD diagnosis, a doctor said I had cerebral palsy. Other doctors did not follow through. I identify myself as Autistic.

It is known that girls are less likely to receive an autism diagnosis. Women might find it difficult, too. Most likely because of society's expectations of how girls should behave, be, or react, we are less likely to be diagnosed and sometimes the diagnosis comes later in life.

This was never an issue for me. Once I received my diagnosis, the fact that I am Autistic was never in doubt, and the doctors agreed.

That was then. Even though the diagnosis was not controversial, growing up was a little more complicated. Several times I was said to be an "atypical" Autistic, maybe because I liked to cuddle, could make eye contact with some people, and liked to stim but not in a way that was considered a "typical autism stim" (I don't know what people meant by that).

The first thing many people thought when they saw me was "mentally retarded." I am non-speaking and did not have a reliable way to communicate. I could make noises and echo a few words, and I could make a light laughing sound. To me, this was communication, but people around me would hear just a lot of nonsense.

It was difficult for me to respond to people's voices. Sometimes it still is. Those times when I could make eye contact with other people, I could not understand the words they were saying. I was focused on their faces. Sometimes I was seeing the words as a colorful, dancing group of letters. It was beautiful and nothing else mattered. When someone said my name, three little letters—green, pink, and yellow—would float around, and it was like music.

My response to people talking to me was, usually, a stare and a smile. Their conclusion: "She can't understand anything." I could, but interaction was hard, and the beauty of the words was much more attractive.

The fact that I would simply smile when talked to was, at least once, "tested" (as witnessed by a friend). A person said something to me, forcing me to look at his face, and I was mesmerized by the words I was seeing. The things he was saying, according to the friend, weren't nice things. Yet, I smiled. His conclusion was, to him, obvious: "Amy is not home, and she does not care."

It went like this: "She is smiling; what a sweet girl. What a shame she cannot understand anything, and she does not care either. She is not Autistic, and if she is, she is 'very' retarded" (language of that time).

All this still happens. From the misconception of my intellectual ability, to my being able to make "good" eye contact, to my not being able to respond to verbal prompts. I still look very disabled and, to some, not "really" Autistic. So, their conclusion is that I have an intellectual disability. Most people, when they learn I am Autistic, will say, "Oh, she is in her own little world then. Poor girl." (Yes, they still call me "girl.")

I have to say that I don't think people who have an intellectual disability are lesser people than Autistic people. I don't know if I am intellectually disabled or not. I don't think anyone knows exactly what this means. I just point out the confusion because I am certain of my Autistic identity, and many people refuse to see that I am, indeed, Autistic.

Here is one thing I wish my parents knew: my world was ever expanding, but I was being pulled back from it because everyone wanted to make me do and react to things as if I could experience them like neurotypicals do. They wanted me to fit into their molds of misconceptions and prejudices. My reactions did not fit the little they knew about autism and Autistic people. They decided that my diagnosis, my identity, was wrong and labeled me with what they believed was a "lower grade."

My parents were exceptionally loving, but the information given to them was not about hope and accomplishments but about tragedy and resignation. They were very close to giving up on seeing me as a person with a future. Luckily, they never gave up. But the path was not easy, and it was full of bumps.

I wish they knew then what they learned later: That autism has gifts, like the words dancing to a symphony of colors and the unique physical sensations each one of them brings. That my smile, my expressions, didn't have anything to do with what people were saying but everything to do with what I—only I—could see. I wish they knew then that my learning process was different, yet efficient, and that I could not learn anything if I was not given the materials and opportunities to try.

This way of experiencing the world should be used for the benefit of Autistics. I believe it facilitates our interactions, expressions, and communication.

When I didn't respond to someone but just stared and smiled, my parents would look down in sadness (ableism was everywhere, including my home. I am glad to report that they've learned and come to value and respect all disabled people). Had they known how connected I was with beauty, how I could absorb knowledge, maybe some of my early experiences would have been less traumatic.

Another misconception I experienced growing up Autistic was the one that assumed functioning labels are accurate and helpful. They are neither. I am a very complex person. I am Autistic, and I have cerebral palsy and epilepsy. The effects of too many seizures, too many hospitalizations, and too much medication resulted in my development being even more delayed.

Autistic people do have developmental delays, some of us in many areas. We take a more wavy and somewhat difficult path to achieve our milestones. It might take longer for us to learn some things the way neurotypicals do, but we do learn them if we have the proper supports. The seizures did prevent me from developing in my own Autistic time. They got in the way and it made what was already difficult to do—develop at the same pace neurotypical kids were developing—even harder.

As I was gaining some skills my typical peers had gained about three years before, a storm of seizures took over my brain.

I had just learnt how to type to communicate and my parents were delighted to see that I was not the tragic child without a future they were told I was. I could finally make choices; my first one was to ask to leave the luxurious institution where I was placed to "make my life less burdensome on my parents, while giving me a chance to experience some form of human life." The doctors were very good at reducing my life to subhuman status.

Because of the terror in my brain, I spent most of the next two years in the ICUs of hospitals, afraid, scared, and feeling lonely. My mother used to tell a story that a nurse heard me speak one night. What did I say? "This place sucks!" I was the only conscious child there. I don't really remember speaking those words. I remember the emotions but not the events. If I really spoke them, that was the only time, in my whole life, that I used spoken words to convey a message. I certainly felt that way. That's how bad that period of my life was.

All that time in hospitals interrupted my life and my development. Every few weeks I was pulled away from my process of learning by uncontrollable, life-threatening seizures. I did less, typed less, and learned less. My development stalled. Not my thinking, though. My brain somehow survived the attacks and I was more and more eager to learn things. My body did not oblige. The trouble I had making my body respond to my will became so bad as to make me feel that, for a few days at a time, I did not have a body. Seizures did that to me.

Slowly, falteringly, I began relearning how to move, how to make my body relate to the environment. I wanted my Autistic, somewhat awkward movements back, even if my Autistic body did not efficiently respond to my Autistic brain. The seizures made me feel like I had a brain that did not recognize my body at all, and this was unbearable.

The two-year ordeal with the hospitalizations, plus the side effects of all the medications, left me in a constant state of tiredness, seemingly unresponsive, almost unable to walk. All this was another reason for doctors and teachers to be certain of my "low-functioning" label. They were so sure of their failed assessment. They couldn't—or didn't want to—see that my brain was still active. Tired, but active.

This is what I wished my parents knew: doctors, teachers, and "experts" didn't know much about autism and about how we process things. They gave me a label that did not require people to expect much of me. I was left to relearn and learn by myself, to understand things and answer to my own questions in my head. To them, I was so damaged that one seizure, or one hundred, would have the same effect. My brain was already so "abnormal," why worry about how painful and debilitating the whole ordeal was? Add to that the doubts about my ability to type, along with a made up, highly publicized controversy about the validity of facilitated communication. I was silenced, silent and alone.

My parents still believed in me, but they fell for the tragedy speech of people with the right credentials. The fearmongering was powerful, even back then. I was to be placed in a special education class since I could not learn much. Because I was "severely impaired" and "very low-functioning," my parents were told to just hope for some basic life skills and a lot of luck for my adult life.

Where I lived, in Florida, the school system was a big failure. I ended up in a group home in another state. Too many promises of a dedicated staff and an appropriate curriculum fell flat. A few people who saw me as more than a label could not really change how I was classified. I lost four years of growth. I typed very little, and I was still being silenced. I did not learn anything from them. I had to pick up on conversations to make sense of the world. Nobody talked to me. They moved me from one class to another, from one therapy to another (I liked music therapy, but the staff did not pick up on that either), from shower to table to bed. I was alone.

All this happened because doctors and other professionals convinced my parents, through fear and pessimistic projections, that I would never be more than a needy child, and that the best they could hope for was that I had a safe place to live.

There are big implications and great damage caused by functioning labels. The first one, and this should be obvious, is that they dehumanize us. No neurotypical person would accept being called "high-functioning" and therefore be expected never to make a mistake, or to be called "low-functioning" and therefore be ignored and belittled.

The second one is how those labels are imposed on us by people who claim expertise yet never really listen to us, and by people who use the labels but have no idea why they do so. Others use the "functioning" labels to separate "them" from "us." They are good, we are bad; they can, we can't.

Being called "low-functioning" and dismissed as a lost cause did enormous harm to my self-esteem. My loving parents were so worried about my future—not how much I could accomplish, but if I could simply have a safe, maybe happy existence—that they accepted that a beautiful place, though full of empty promises, would be satisfactory to me. They were fooled by the fear dumped on them.

I was still typing/talking with them and they knew how I felt. But their fear prevented them from seeing and hearing me. They did not presume my competence, not when it came to big decisions about my life. I could make choices, chose my food and what to wear. But they were led to believe that I could not really know things, have dreams, or analyze. I wasn't "that smart."

I know they struggled to reconcile this lack of presumption of competence with some of the decisions they made. After all, I was typing very insightful thoughts. I don't blame them. The belief that a life with a lot of schedules for meaningless activities would be more beneficial for me was mainstream, and the school system continued to fail me. Besides, back then, there were no Autistic role models. But I wish they had known that I was very aware of everything and that they had not trusted so much in the neurotypical definition of me.

Another thing I wish my parents knew when I was growing up is this: my facial expressions are deceiving, and my ability to empathize makes me act against my own good.

I have been, for the most part, a quiet and, according to many, "sweet" person. Until a few years ago, I had not even typed or thought about words like "empowerment," "self-determination," or "self-advocacy." I would just hope for understanding and a happy outcome.

In difficult situations, even in abusive ones, I just smiled. It was not a real smile, but that was what everyone saw. Or I would do my best to disconnect from reality and lose myself in lights and colors, reacting to the outside world as if I were on automatic pilot.

Of course, that was one more reason for people to say that I couldn't understand or feel anything, or that I didn't care.

Once, with second-degree burns on my arm, and in a lot of pain, someone looked at me and, seeing no expression of pain, said that I "did not feel pain." I do, but my face does not show the intensity of the pain, or my reactions might not be what neurotypical people expect.

I used to, and still do, think about other people's feelings before my own well-being. I thought about my parents' struggle with the system to find a decent school for me, so I did not tell them that I was not practicing typing, that my days were full of empty commands to be followed to nowhere, that I was bored and that my brain was not being challenged. I knew they would feel bad and frustrated, so I did not say anything. I had too much empathy for them. I did not know how to self-advocate.

I thought about my doctors and teachers, and how much smarter and knowledgeable everyone believed they were, about how they were trying to help me, so I never told anyone that they were bad professionals. I knew some of them were good in their hearts and I did not want to hurt them.

Empathy and my "sweet nature," my not knowing I had rights, and the years of people saying I was so broken made me an easy target for abuse and compliant behavior. My facial expressions made it "clear," to people who thought they knew it all, that I was not a sentient, intelligent being.

I wish my parents knew that. They would not have stopped looking for better places where I could learn. They would have tried to lift me up.

I am telling these events about my life because I think it is important to know that Autistics do not process and react to things like neurotypicals do, and that this can be to our detriment, even when we are surrounded with love.

With all the negativity directed at us and at our neurology, we need good role models who have had similar experiences to help us, and who truly support us, to teach us how to cope and how to fight against the barriers and toward acceptance.

I have learned that. But I have not changed a lot. I still smile when upset, I still look serious when typing or reading a joke, and I still have not learned, or am not able to perform, so-called basic skills. I do speak (type) out more, and I connect more. I am learning to say "no" and to choose my friends more carefully.

That's what I wish my parents knew: that community and role models are the best source for a happy Autistic outcome.

They did not have access to Autistic role models back then. But parents today do. And we Autistic adults are here to help. We know things about Autistic neurology that no neurotypical can even begin to guess. We can help every child be assured that they are worthy and perfect. This and parental love are key to a growing process with confidence and possibilities.

I had all the love, yet it was not an easy ride. I had to go through bumps and pain. I was misunderstood, mislabeled, mistreated. I lost time, I lost opportunities, I had to race, and I fell behind.

I wish everyone knew that unless our voices count, the bad events that happened to me will happen again. It does not have to be this way. As I said, my parents eventually learned the things that would help me. Not without mistakes, but we all succeeded in our journey together. My mother was my loudest cheerleader, and my father, today, follows me in my activism. Their trust, acceptance, and support help and encourage me to keep being the best me I can be.

I wish they knew that I would find my voice, my community, and my purpose. They lacked resources back then. Parents today can know a lot more and help their Autistic child's path be much less bumpy.

19 The View from Outside the Window

HW

I needed help to shift from that tiny worldview to the big airplane view.

———

WHEN I WAS CLEANING OUT my room one day, I was immediately drawn to my old pile of journals. It was astonishing to remember how I used to be and feel. It's sad to think about, but at one time I almost lost all of my creativity, particularly my ability to write, as a young adult. I had been writing for as long as I can remember, since childhood. As an Autistic person, writing came naturally to me and was an easy way to cope. Unfortunately, I was depressed a lot, and this really blocked my creative thinking. This was frightening to me and I began to self-censor everything I said or wrote. My old journals have huge gaps in them because I tore out everything that didn't fit my standards.

My love of writing was unexpectedly rekindled when a teacher noticed my potential and told me that I was a great writer, which encouraged me to start writing again. I wish I could thank her for that, since it helped me get through one of the worst periods of my life. It was one of the few times I wrote and didn't self-censor. It was one of the few times I didn't feel like I had to please someone. The words escaped from inside of me in jumbles and messy writing. It was what I could never say to my parents or counselors.

Just like I struggled to see value in my writing, I didn't fully accept that I was okay with being Autistic until later in life. I was extremely inexperienced with my new self-acceptance. It wasn't always the best feeling because I didn't know how to handle this kind of freedom. I guess even as a kid I knew that something would change, but I was scared. Out of fear and denial, I'd constantly rebuke people who thought I could be a leader, but in my prayers, written out in tiny cursive bubble writing, I prayed to be bolder so that I could one day lead. Some people really liked me exercising my freedom, but others absolutely hated it! I guess I was a bit too excited and outspoken.

While drinking coffee with one of my favorite professors recently, I thought about how much my worldview has shifted. The social model of disability talks about breaking down attitudinal and environmental barriers. How many people have their own internalized ableism and internal barriers? Ableism is the attitude that favors nondisabled people, and it is systemic. What are your own barriers? On the other side is the medical model: the belief that people have to be fixed and that doctors know best. I am all for medical care, but I don't feel like I need to be fixed at all. Way too often we are told we have to be a certain way in order to comply with society. Too often, even people with disabilities begin to absorb the ableism around us.

I look forward to the day when I won't have to light a candle for a life lost due to ableism, like I have to do every year now. I constantly have to tune my ears to catch ableism. And yes, ableism is as real as racism and sexism, but it is a kind of discrimination that sneaks up behind you, and somehow people view it as acceptable. Like cigarette smoke snaking around you, or some colorless gas, it is seductive in the way it works. It is appealing but toxic, and it can kill you internally. It can lead to horrible external things, including abuse, betrayal, and murder. It makes me heavy-hearted to think of how many examples I can think of where this has happened. Words are powerful, so please don't use discriminatory words. Please don't add to the exchange of ableism.

For me, self-acceptance was similar to a feeling that one of my queer friends described about coming to terms with their sexuality. My friend said that instead of feeling like they were being forced "out of a closet" into the open without any help, it felt more like a change in perspective. It's like when an airplane rises off the ground. Like going from seeing only your small world and thinking that every part of the world is exactly like yours until you leave your little corner. Leaving the tarmac, the plane starts soaring, and you look down from the window and see how tiny your little world really is. That's what self-acceptance seemed like for me. It was that kind of a cathartic relief, realizing that my view from before was so limited and now being able to realize what life could be like.

Sometimes I wonder if that is how my parents felt when they realized I was Autistic . . . that a huge part of their lives shifted from one small view to looking out the window of a plane and seeing all the small patches of land underneath the sky. It's kind of an overwhelming feeling, to be honest, and I fear that some people might even call it an identity crisis or a death sentence. I find it sad that some parents won't embrace their child's autism or, if the child is the one who can't handle being Autistic, they choose to stay in their small world of familiarity in fear of what they might see outside the window of the airplane in their own life.

When I think back about my writing, I notice something. All the fictional characters I wrote about as a kid were what I wanted to be subconsciously even though I wasn't aware at the time! I needed help to shift from that tiny worldview to the big airplane view in order to see out the window. Some people refuse to ever see out that window or even get on the airplane at all. To think that I almost was one of them! Today, I don't think I could ever forgive myself if I had allowed fear to prevent me from getting on that plane. It gave me a whole new world perspective, and I would never trade the moment when identifying as capital "A" Autistic and capital "D" Disabled became part of my life. This is a source of pride for me. I know I'm more than Autistic, of course, but it is still important to me.[1]

20 Finding Me: The Journey to Acceptance

Morénike Giwa Onaiwu

Little Morénike, so, so strange
Overly anxious at the prospect of change

Tiny hands flapping as she averts her gaze
Twirling and spinning, as if in a daze

Hyperlexic days, echolalic nights
Migraines and meltdowns caused by fluorescent lights

Or by a certain texture, smell, taste, or sound
They disturb her so much that she simply shuts down

The way that she thinks . . . it's so very literal
And the way she behaves is almost like a ritual

Things must be done in a particular way
Or else she is unable to cope with her day

Social cues elude her; inferences too
So very smart, yet she doesn't have a clue

Naive and trusting, she's a manipulator's prey
Easy to fool because she believes what you say

Languishing in a world whose rules are unspoken
She is perceived as defective and broken

One simple word could create a cataclysm
Of understanding, of acceptance. That word is "autism"

A six-letter word that could have helped to explain
That there was absolutely nothing wrong with her brain

But the words do not come. She remains unseen
'Cause she doesn't fit the profile . . . know what I mean?

She's not of the gender and not of the race
That's associated with autism in that time and space

An Xennial growing up in-between DSM III and IV
Her autism presents in a way that they're not looking for

Plus, her IQ is high, and she has the ability to speak
So she isn't perceived as disabled . . . just as a freak

She learns how to mimic, to mask, to hide
She suppresses herself at all times—to survive

Her family lovingly tries to affirm her worth
Asserts that she has always been different—since birth

"You are unique," they tell her. "Be proud!
Never hide who you are; live your life out loud."

But how can she believe the kind words her family has spoken
When the rest of the world has shown her she's hopelessly broken?

So she somnambulates through years of her life, in despair
Choking beneath the mask of "normalcy" she must always wear

Over the years her unshed tears well up inside
Accompanied by a growing yearning for suicide

As a possible antidote to the pain
That flows as readily as the blood in her veins

But a truth that's unknown does not cease to be
It watches quietly in the dark for a chance to break free

And though her despair seems incessantly vast
The day is coming that she shall be free—at last

It happens by accident when she is all grown
She's now an adult with kids of her own

Her daughter is diagnosed with autism; her son too
Providers frequently remark, "The kids are so much like you."

She builds up the courage to seek her own evaluation
When she receives the results, she is filled with elation

The paper states "299.00, F 84.0, Level One."
In other words . . . she's on the autism spectrum

Not a freak of nature; not a monstrosity
Merely a person with unique neurology

If only she'd known about this way back then
She wondered how different her life may have been

But the past is gone, and nothing we can say
Can change what has happened; we must live for today

And though some parts of her life are still tough
She's doing her best, and that's more than enough

Little Morénike grew up and survived. She is proof
That life can be transformed when you're living your truth.

21 Autism, Self-Acceptance, and Hope

Lynne Soraya

You are what you are, and what you are is just as worthy as anyone else.

IN THE YEARS that I've been active in the online autism community, I've had the opportunity to interact with a number of parents, to answer their questions, and to hear their fears. What I hear from them often concerns me deeply. Because what I hear is often filled with so much fear. And so much of the popular discourse around autism seems to feed that fear. I find that deeply sad because I feel it does not need to be this way.

I grew up without a diagnosis, facing a lot of confusion and pain because I didn't understand my own neurology. I didn't understand why people could do things that I couldn't. I didn't understand why some things were so painful for me. That ignorance had really painful consequences, leading me to believe that there was something deeply, deeply wrong with me. I lived with self-hatred for years.

Yet even with those consequences there are times when I think I was better off *not* knowing. Why is that? Well, when I hear the things that parents and children are told today, the way the label is often used to limit, I wonder what that would've meant for the life I live today. This is something I had to navigate my way through when I first learned I was on the spectrum, now almost fifteen years ago.

You see, by that point in my life, I had already done any number of things that many of the articles I read claimed I never should have been able to do. I was in a long-term relationship and was soon to be married. I had a steady job where people seemed to like me and where I received high performance ratings consistently. Through the social demands of my soon-to-be husband's work, I found myself socializing with senior executives and CEOs of large organizations.

The people who knew me, the people I worked with, might've thought I was eccentric or odd, but I don't know that they would have made the connection to autism. But I had learned at that point how to mask my challenges, my anxieties, and my fears so well that even my husband and family didn't really realize they existed. I'd learned how to "pass," but at a great cost to myself.

The unfortunate fact of passing is that you can never be sure that people who claim to like you really do. If they could see you as you really are, as you are when all the barriers go down and you just don't have the energy to pretend anymore, would they still like what they saw? That was the reality I lived with every day, and the fact that people *did* like the false self that I presented seemed only to underscore the deep insecurities and self-hatred that I'd learned to feel. It seemed they liked the false me better than the real me.

So, when my "Aha!" moment really came, my first thought was, "Oh good, now that I know what it is, I can fix it!" Now that I knew what the problem was, I could make myself into the person that other people wanted me to be. I could make my false front real. I dove into the autism literature, read the books, looked up research, listened to podcasts, and visited every site that claimed to have some solution or cure to give. But the result of all this was something unexpected.

As I read the explanations that many of these so-called experts provided, they didn't make sense. What they claimed to be the motive behind many autistic behaviors didn't coincide at all with my actual experience. In fact, they were often polar opposites of my reality. And then there was the negativity. I read that I was supposed to be "soulless." That just being around me was damaging to the people I loved. That my life was a burden on other people's and that I "sucked the life" from other people like a vampire. That unless I could become "indistinguishable from my peers" I couldn't be successful, couldn't be loved, couldn't find friends. That my life would be a tragedy.

In the meantime, here I was. In many ways I was indistinguishable from my peers, but my life felt empty. It felt like a fraud. For every compliment I got on what I did well, there was a secret voice inside that said, "You wouldn't think that about me if you really knew." The only person who did know to some extent was the man who would be my husband. Yet even he struggled to reconcile the two sides of me. He'd seen my struggles, yet he'd seen enough of my successes that it was hard for him to sort out which of them was the real me. In the end, even I didn't know.

But, beneath all the self-hatred and the identity crisis, there was the survivalist part of my psyche, the core of self-esteem that still remained. It was that part of my psyche that finally turned things around, that surfaced one day while I was reading the website of a cure-based organization and assimilating all of the things I was supposed to be, with tears running down my face. It said, "That's not right. You are who you are, and what you are is just as worthy as anybody else."

Around the same time, I started reading books and blogs by others on the spectrum. Their writings told a completely different story, one more in tune with my actual experience. They described experiences I'd shared and motivations I recognized. But they had something I didn't have, and that was self-acceptance. I read about their challenges and their successes and the ways they had learned to navigate through some of the challenges that I hadn't yet figured out. I began to build a sense of self-understanding, and I came to a realization: After all those years of seeing myself as a broken "normal" person, I realized I wasn't broken it all. I was a perfectly whole and valuable autistic person.

During this time in my life, I made great strides forward in my goals. I found myself in a job in which I often represented my company in the community, a role that would seem to have demanded skills I shouldn't have (according to the experts), and yet I did very well. I did so because I now understood the differences between myself and those who weren't autistic, and that knowledge allowed me to adapt my approach and educate others so that my behavior was not misinterpreted. It opened up a whole new area of emotional intimacy with my husband, because the point of acceptance was that I could talk about the things I feared, struggled with, and worried about, without shame. I didn't have to hide anymore.

I began to write about my experiences, something I had always done to make sense of things. Putting things on paper seemed to make my thoughts and feelings coalesce in ways that they didn't seem to do for me verbally or when they were just in my head. Through doing so, I began to wonder: If others' stories were so meaningful to me, would mine be equally meaningful to other people? I didn't know, but I spent some time thinking about it. If I was writing about these issues anyway, why not share them? Perhaps others might learn something from my process. What resulted was amazing for me. The level of support and caring available from so many people in the autism community still staggers me. I can only hope that my writings give to others as much as others have given to me.

To date, what my journey has taught me is that acceptance of yourself is crucial. Believing that autistic traits are "bad" while the rest of you is "good" makes it more difficult to deal with the challenges those traits may present in a social environment than if you're able to accept them and see them clearly for what they are. And once you've had some time to assess where you are, what your skills and abilities look like, you'll find you can't really separate the autism from the rest. It is an integral part of what you are. For me, the things that have caused me the most struggle are also the things that have given me the most joy. That being the case, what would my life look like if I tried to eliminate those traits?

When people talk about "negative" autistic traits, one trait they often talk about is sensory sensitivity. It can be painful. It certainly has caused me great pain over the years, especially when I didn't understand what it was or why I struggled so much with noises, tactile sensations, etc. Yet I love music, and music has been one of the most crucial tools I've used over the years to keep myself calm, grounded, and happy. When I'm overwhelmed, listening to a song I like can turn me around in an instant. And really, what is music? It is sound. Just as I react painfully to someone whistling nearby, a single note or chord in a piece of music can touch me deeply and bring me to tears. Both are forms of sensitivity to a sensory stimulus: sound. There are two sides to a coin. I can't eliminate one without eliminating the other. Thus, I can't say that sensory issues are inherently bad or inherently good. They simply are.

Given this reality, what does a successful life look like for someone like me? To me, a successful life requires assessing my skills and abilities and the things that cause me discomfort or pain and finding ways to work with that profile of skills and abilities, rather than against them. Fighting who you are is often futile, and the result is that you expend so much time fighting what you don't like, that you don't focus on the skills and abilities that you have in abundance. Success on the spectrum often means doing things differently than others might expect. Having the openness to be able to admit to things that others might judge and see them impartially is a skill that is absolutely required to make that happen. It is that clarity that allows you to see the ways you can adapt your path to work for your specific neurology.

When I look back at my life, many of my successes can be tied to things that others might identify as autistic traits. My visual thinking and the way I process things allows me to see things in systems and processes with the speed and clarity that others can't. My memory allows me to "connect the dots" between current and past conversations that others have long forgotten. My tendency to become engrossed in topics that others thought were arcane led me to develop special skills that were in demand, and it provided me the perseverance and impetus to continue growing and learning when others were happy with the status quo. My natural tendency to analyze sometimes allows me to predict others' behavior more accurately than they can themselves. I approach things in a differ-ent way, and that is a strength, but I can only see this through a lens of self-acceptance.

This reality is part of what troubles me when I hear what par-ents are told by some professionals and groups, and when I so often hear the false dichotomy of autism as something to fight but the person as being something to accept. It's taken nearly fifteen years of deep self-reflection for me to fully realize the duality of most of the traits that I have. It's easy to look at the surface and say that you see no redeeming value in a particular trait, but it may be there if you look. Sometimes it's hiding in plain sight, just as my love of music was for years. It takes a lot of experience to draw those parallels. A lot of us have only begun making those connections in adulthood.

Likewise, such a message makes it all too easy to set up the type of self-loathing I lived with for years. I didn't have a diagnosis then. I didn't have commercials on TV providing a list of my traits and calling them something bad. My parents weren't itemizing them on blog posts on the web for everyone to see and discussing the things they've done to battle them. I couldn't get on the web and read the websites of major organizations talking about me as a burden and a tragedy, saying that my family "wasn't living" because of me. Yet, I still picked up on the negative messages that the world had about autism and the traits that define it. I picked it up through teasing and implicit judgments: The subtle rejections that happened ev-ery day. The friends who began avoiding me or stopped calling or coming over to play. The teachers who jumped to conclusions that my behaviors were the result of some horrific abuse rather than an attempt to solve a problem in a less than optimal way.

How much easier is it to come to the conclusion that you are broken, "lesser than," when you are faced with these messages ev-ery day? When you hear people around you talking about how sad it is that you were born instead of a so-called "normal" child? This is what worries me, because when I imagine myself as a child hearing these messages, I can only imagine what would've been the depth of my despair. And with that lack of hope, I wonder if I would have accomplished the things that I've accomplished. I wonder if I would have the life that I have or if I would have just knuckled under and believed the things that were being said about me.

I imagine my mother and father being given percentages, predictions of what I wouldn't be able to do, and how that lens would have changed how they looked at me. My parents and teachers always started from the perspective of what I could do versus what I couldn't. What would my life have been like had they started from the opposite assumption? I've experienced enough of that in the world to know the frustrations of having your abilities discounted and looked down upon even when you know your own potential. When I visualize that happening on a daily basis, it makes me deeply sad.

Doctors are not magicians or soothsayers. They can't predict the future any more than anyone else can. So, don't let your child's life be limited by their predictions. Teach her how to accept herself; help her look for her strengths and capitalize on them. Autism should not be something that someone is ashamed of or afraid of; it is simply a profile of skills and abilities that a person must work with in life, and that description of those skills and abilities is a tool to use in building self-understanding. This is what I wish all parents would know.

Fear is the enemy. Hope is everything. Acceptance is how it happens.

Intersectional Identity
and Finding Community

22 Keep Her Safe; Let Her Fly Free

Maxfield Sparrow

Teach your daughter to own her body.

WHEN I WAS IN MIDDLE SCHOOL, the bullying I had been subject to for the last six or seven years suddenly took on a sexual tone. The girls bullied me by spreading rumors that I was having sex, by calling me sexual names, including ones I didn't even understand yet, by drawing obscene pictures of me or writing obscene notes about me and passing them around the room so that they would make their way to me, then giggling when I saw them. One girl even shoved me out the fire door, naked, when we were changing clothes for gym class.

The boys bullied me too, but in a different way. I got pulled into niches beneath the stairs or little alcoves behind the lockers where I would be groped or kissed against my will—disgusting, wet kisses with tongue.

I didn't tell my parents what was happening. I didn't tell anyone what was happening. I endured it all with shame and a sense of self-loathing because I thought I deserved it. Why would I think something so ridiculous as that? Because of what my parents had told me for years.

I am telling you about the humiliation I lived through so that you can understand what your role is in preventing your child from going through something similar. I know that sex can be a difficult topic, especially for a parent. It's hard for many parents to think of their child growing up and becoming consensually sexual and almost impossible to think of their sexuality being infringed upon in unwanted ways. But it is a very important topic, and when

I think about what I want parents of Autistic girls in particular to know, issues of sexuality top the list.

So, what was my parents' role in my decision to keep my sexual shame a secret? It all goes back to how they responded to the bullying I had been facing for years before the sexual abuses at school began. When I would come home crying about how I was being treated, my parents told me that it was my fault. They said I was bringing the bullying on myself by insisting on being different from everyone else. They did not understand or accept that being different from others was beyond my control. They did not believe me when I said I wished I were like everyone else. They blamed me, not the bullies, for being a victim of bullying.

When the bullying turned sexual, I assumed it was more of the same: my fault. I was afraid to tell anyone because I already felt shame about the things people were saying and doing to me. I assumed that if I told anyone, they would just agree with the others and increase my shame and sorrow. So, I kept it secret and tried my best to avoid everyone—an impossible goal when you're locked up together inside a school building. I begged to be homeschooled, but my mother refused. I had been a "behavior problem" for years, and she said, "Why should I reward your bad behavior by letting you stay home from school?" So, again, the problem was all my fault, and I was left to suffer at the hands of others with the conviction that it was only what I deserved. Those were nightmare years for me.

So, I want you to understand that if you want your daughter to feel like the door is open for her to come to you to talk about sexual issues (and I do hope that is what you want!), your openness starts many years earlier. How you respond to non-sexual problems in your daughter's life will set the tone for what she will expect if she comes to you with a sexual problem. Do you shout when she doesn't do her homework? Do you nag at her not to flap her hands or walk on tiptoe or spin around? Do you dismiss her concerns when other children treat her harshly? Do you force her to apologize when she has conflict with others, regardless of how she feels about offering an apology? These are the sorts of interactions that are paving the way for a future where she fears to approach you to discuss a sexual issue.

You also want to indicate that you are open to talking about sexuality specifically. I know this can be really hard for some parents, but it's crucial. My parents were very uncomfortable about sexuality, and that discomfort came through loud and clear to me. For example, once I put some old clothes to be donated to charity into a big cardboard box I got from behind the grocery store and set it in the living room to wait for other contributions to be added. My father got upset and demanded the box be removed from his sight. I asked if it was because it made the living room look messy and he said, "No, it's because. . . . because. . . . of what's written on it!" and he left the room. I looked at the box and it said, "Kotex." He was so uncomfortable with the thought of menstruation that he could not even bear to look at a cardboard box with a tampon brand name on it.

My mother tried to give me sexual information at puberty, but she did it by handing me a small stack of books and saying I should read them and come to her if I had any questions afterward. I am not very good at reading tones of voice most of the time, but it was clear even to me that her tone of voice was saying, "Please don't have any questions! Just read the books and don't talk to me about it!"

That backfired on her, though, because the books never mentioned that the first menstruation can be (pardon the mental image I'm about to give you) kind of brown and gummy. Mine didn't look how I expected; I was waiting for blood to come. Blood is a bright red liquid. When I saw a sort of mud coming out of me, I was terrified! I thought I had cancer or something! I mean, I can laugh about it now, but I genuinely thought I was dying, and I was so afraid that I couldn't speak. I went to my mother with some of the "mud" on a piece of toilet tissue and just held it up for her to see. I couldn't make words at all. It was one of the most horrible and frightening experiences of my life, and the books did not prepare me for it. My mother was disgusted and impatient with me—in fairness, since I wasn't speaking, she may not have realized how scared I was—and hustled me back to the bathroom to hand me a pad and then rushed away with no reassurance or explanation.

Don't let your daughter go through something like that. Make sure she knows you are okay with talking about sex. And if you aren't okay talking about sex, it's time to start getting okay with it. Do whatever you have to do: read books, talk to yourself in the mirror until you can do it without shame, but really work hard on this because your daughter will need you to be there for her, and she will need you to communicate with more than just your words that all these things that are happening with her body and her mind are okay and natural and nothing to fear.

If you want your child to grow up healthy and happy and safe, you need to create an environment where they feel comfortable with their sexuality and where they feel allowed to own their body and sexuality. There is a sort of autism therapy, compliance therapy, that goes under many names, but the end goal is to ensure compliance with adult demands at the expense of the needs and emotional well-being of the patient. You will want to watch out for it because it is very dangerous to all Autistics and, in our culture, especially dangerous to female Autistics.

Let me talk for a moment about one very popular type of compliance therapy, behavioral momentum, and then I will explain why it is so dangerous and suggest an alternative.

Behavioral momentum is a type of therapy that seeks to increase compliance. As described by behavior analyst Dr. Teka J. Harris, then director of the May Institute, it is similar to playing the children's game "Simon Says." In that game, participants are asked to do simple things like raise a hand or take a step forward. By requesting many simple tasks in a row, each one prefaced by the phrase "Simon says," the game leader lulls the players into a state of compliance where they are accustomed to following directions. When the game leader then makes a request but does not preface it by saying "Simon says," many of the players will automatically obey the command anyway, even though they know they are not supposed to comply if the leader does not say "Simon says."

Behavioral momentum uses this natural human tendency towards compliance after a series of easy-to-follow requests that lull the Autistic into automatically complying with a request the Autistic person is resistant to. Dr. Harris says, "An individual may refuse to complete a task for a variety of reasons: the task may be too complex; a physical limitation may hinder completion of the task; or he or she may lack confidence. Regardless of the reason for non-compliant behavior, behavior analysts have a strategy to deal with it—behavioral momentum."[1]

Re-read what I just quoted from Dr. Harris. That statement alarms me and, if you want to be more in tune with how your child experiences the world, that statement should alarm you, too. Dr. Harris bluntly says that it doesn't matter why the child doesn't want to complete a task. It could be too complex, it could be physically impossible, it could be frightening or overwhelming—none of that matters. All that matters is using a strategy to trick the child into doing it anyway.

This is key to my alternative suggestion: Don't try to trick your child into doing what you want them to do. Become a detective and find out why they don't want to do it. They may have a perfectly good reason. It might be dangerous for them to do it. Don't assume that you know better than your child just because you are the grown-up and you are not Autistic. Listen to your child and work to understand why they don't want to do something before you force them into it.

A perfect example of an Autistic child being non-compliant for a good reason is the story of the day that Emma refused to get off the school bus. Emma's mother, Ariane Zurcher, tells the story on her blog, *Emma's Hope Book*.[2] Emma was going to go to a new school. Her mother explained everything to her. Emma was ready. But the bus driver didn't understand and, instead, began driving to the old school.

Emma, who was ten years old at the time, said it was the wrong way. No one listened. Emma shouted that it was the wrong way. Again, no one listened! The adults assumed they knew better and when Emma refused to get off the bus, they treated it as an instance of non-compliance. When the bus driver finally called home to complain to Emma's parents, they straightened everything out: Emma was right to be non-compliant because the situation was wrong, and Emma knew better than the adults around her. Her parents were understandably overjoyed and praised Emma for advocating for herself.

The story of Emma refusing to get off the bus illustrates perfectly why it is more important to understand why an Autistic child does not want to do something than it is to try to force them to comply with what the adults want them to do. Now imagine a child who doesn't want to comply because of a serious problem. Maybe the child doesn't want to hug a family member because the child doesn't like hugs or doesn't feel like hugging right now, or maybe that family member has been doing something inappropriate with the child. Isn't it more important to find out why your child doesn't want to hug someone than it is to force them to hug? It is better to respect the child's right to decide what they do with their body and who they show affection to than it is to force them to hug someone so they won't be rude or hurt someone's feelings. Your child's sense of owning her body is more important than offending someone by not touching them!

And that is where the real danger of compliance therapies comes in. Compliance therapies that do not care why a child is not complying are teaching your child that she does not own her body and that she is not allowed to make her own decisions. What makes behavioral momentum particularly insidious is that it models the way young boys attempt to encourage young girls to engage in sexual activity before they are ready.

Now don't think that I'm trying to demonize boys here. I'm not. But sexual urges can be very strong, and some (not all!) boys will resort to all kinds of manipulation to try to gain access to a girl's sexuality. I'm reminded of a scene from a movie that I saw so many years ago that I can no longer recall what movie it was. A young couple sat in a car, watching a movie together at a drive-in theater. The boy put his hand on the girl's shoulder and asked, "Do you trust me?" She smiled and said, "Yes." He moved his hand to her upper chest. "Do you trust me?" Again, she responded, "Yes." He moved his hand partway into the top of her blouse. "Do you trust me?" . . . Do you see what he is doing? It is behavioral momentum in action!

If you allow your daughter to be treated with behavioral momentum—or, really, any compliance therapy—that disregards the need to discover why she is not complying, you are training her to say yes again and again, no matter where the boy moves his hand and no matter how she really feels about his hand being there.

As if that weren't horrifying enough, behavioral momentum and similar compliance therapies are taking unfair advantage of a feature of the Autistic brain. We experience, in varying degrees from person to person, something that we Autistics have come to call "Autistic inertia." A simple definition of inertia in physics is that objects at rest tend to stay at rest and objects in motion tend to stay in motion unless acted on by an outside force. In a way, we are like those objects. We can have a hard time switching gears. When we have difficulty starting our homework, it's not always laziness or simple resistance. Sometimes we really want to do our homework but need help switching gears from what we are already doing. Sometimes we get started with our homework and then get stuck there and can't stop. I have spent twenty hours straight researching a topic for a paper. Even after I knew I had enough material to begin writing the paper, I couldn't switch gears to move from researching to writing, so I just kept on going, hour after hour, until I collapsed from hunger and exhaustion.

Behavioral momentum takes advantage of Autistic inertia to get our brain's gears turning in one direction and then uses our difficulty in switching directions to steer us right into disaster. I would like to see new therapies that don't manipulate and abuse our gear-shifting difficulties but rather work to help us learn how to shift our own gears and how to overcome or work with our Autistic inertia. Autistics who learn to work with our inertia in positive ways accomplish amazing things. We are dedicated and hard workers; help us learn to master that tendency and harness it for our own good.

Behavioral momentum and similar therapies do the opposite of that: they train us to become victims of our Autistic inertia. And when someone comes along who naturally coaxes others by using momentum techniques like I described from that movie scene, we are primed to play right into their hands. Teach your daughter to own her body. Teach your daughter to listen to her instincts. Teach your daughter how to say "no"—and how to mean "no" and how to enforce "no"—beginning from an early age. Do not train your daughter to mindlessly comply with what others wish from her.

You may think that I am saying to let your child run amok and always expect to get what they want. I am not. Help your child understand what society expects from people. Help your child to understand how others feel and how to balance what others want and need with what they want and need. But also help your child to know that it's not okay to let people hurt them. Too many of the standard autism therapies out there don't really care what your child wants and needs. They care what she looks like and they care about how easy she is to "manage." Don't let those therapies "manage" her straight into victimhood.

There's one last thing I want to talk to you about, with respect to your daughter's sexuality. Do not make assumptions. Your daughter may grow up to be sexual and want to date men. She may want to wear a lacy wedding dress, and she may want to have and raise children. But do not assume that she will grow up that way, and be careful not to give her messages that these are the only ways she can be if she wants your love and support.

Autistic females sometimes grow up transgender and choose to take steps to live as a male. Autistic females sometimes grow up to be lesbian, bisexual, pansexual, or asexual. Autistic females sometimes decide to never have children. Autistic females sometimes grow up to be heterosexual females who do not wear makeup or shave their legs. Just like non-Autistic females grow up to express their sexuality in many different ways, Autistic females can develop specific, personal, and sometimes complex sexual and gender identities.

Give your daughter room to grow into the person she truly is. Do not try to cage her into what you think a female ought to be. Do not try to steer her into being mainstream solely due to your fear that life is already hard enough for an Autistic and that a non-mainstream sexual identity would just add to that burden. What will add to the burden of being Autistic in a society that does not understand us is also having a non-mainstream identity but feeling forced to suppress and hide it from everyone—particularly from the people who ought to be most supportive, one's parents.

You don't have to teach your daughter to be "different." Simply allowing her to have access to the many role models out there is enough. When your daughter sees that author and scientist Dr. Temple Grandin is openly asexual or that anthropologist Dr. Dawn Prince-Hughes is both Autistic and an open lesbian (and the first Seattle Miss Leather as well!) or that author and educator Dr. Liane Holliday-Wiley grew up to marry and have children, she will understand that Autistic women can grow up to have many different identities and that this is okay. She will not need you to tell her this specifically if the books written by these Autistic women (and others!) are available for her to read. Encourage your daughter to read autobiographies written by as many different Autistic women as you can. It is good for her to understand the community and culture of those who share her neurotype as she is growing up and seeking to understand where she fits in to this big and often confusing world.

And the final piece of advice I would leave you with is completely unnecessary. Love your child. I don't really need to tell you that because I know you already do. You are reading this book of essays written by Autistic people because you love your child and want to do everything you can to help them grow up strong and healthy.

But I will say it anyway because it is the most important ingredient in raising your child: love them and make sure they always know that you love them. We Autistic people aren't always good at what they call "reading between the lines." Don't make your child struggle to see your love. Make your love explicit in your words and actions. If you raise your child so that they know beyond a shadow of a doubt that they are loved and treasured always and unconditionally, everything else will flow from that, and you will most surely raise a child who is strong and healthy and confident in every way.

23 Tell Me I'm Autistic

Anonymous

We're looking in the wrong places, trying to be what we think we're supposed to be or what society has told us we have to be, and coming up short every time.

━━━━━━━

ONE OF THE MOST profound things that happened to me in my life, aside from the birth of my three beautiful children, was learning that I was Autistic. After my son was diagnosed, I did quite a lot of research to confirm what I had been told. And because I love research, you could probably call it my "special interest." During that time, I found myself learning, not about things I had never heard but of things I already knew: behaviors, mannerisms, characteristics, or the ominous-sounding "red flags" and "warning signs." *The names alone scared me!* I was reading about things I knew very well from a personal standpoint. The more I read about autism, *the more I saw myself.*

My son was a late diagnosis, not because I was in denial, but because I didn't see his characteristics as all that different. Aside from his being non-speaking and having developmental disabilities, we approached life in very similar manners. Long story short, my self-diagnosis came shortly after my son's, and my formal diagnosis by a professional two years later. My daughter's autism diagnosis soon followed. My youngest daughter, while having other disabilities, is beginning to show signs of autism as well. She has yet to be evaluated, but like myself and my other two children we will allow her to grow into the person she is supposed to be. If she is Autistic—*excellent!* If she is not Autistic—*excellent!* Neurodiversity is a beautiful thing!

I want to address an extremely important topic, one that, had I known as a child, would have changed my life dramatically. When I was invited to submit a piece for AWN, I was both honored and ecstatic. I love AWN! And when I learned the topic: *What do I wish every parent of an Autistic girl knew?* I had a hundred things race through my mind at once: hygiene, puberty, relationships, social interaction, friendships, self-perception, and on and on. And then it dawned on me that all of these things and so much more depend on the one thing I was never told as a child . . .

That I was Autistic.

I grew up in the 1970s and '80s. Autism was not the headliner it is today. There was no talk of a spectrum. No discussion of differentiation or neurodiversity. Society had a very clear definition of what it considered autism, and that was depicted in the highly acclaimed 1988 film *Rain Man*. I was nothing like the man in the film; therefore, I was not Autistic. I was shy, withdrawn, nervous, and anxious, and I had learning difficulties. I was also confused by social interactions and relationships. But like many Autistics I know, I learned to mask my disabilities at a very young age so I could pass *(act like everyone else)*. By the time I was a freshman in college, I was experiencing OCD, insomnia, chronic migraines, and chronic panic attacks (which I learned later were actually meltdowns), and I was in the hospital undergoing a multitude of diagnostic tests, including CT scans for brain tumors. My neurology was never in question. I was able to go to school, make good grades, and be a very social person. On the outside, I was society's version of a "good kid." On the inside, however, I was a mess.

From a young age, around five years old, I was hiding in my room experiencing what I later learned were meltdowns and self-injurious behavior (biting myself, pulling my hair, and hitting myself, walls, furniture). I lived in a constant state of worry, frustration, and anger, and I never told anyone. I was too scared.

As a child, I was painfully aware that there was something "wrong" with me. So, while growing up, I worked diligently to hide my thoughts and feelings and the confusion that was ever present.

By the time I was in high school, I wrestled daily with extremely low self-esteem. While I had no problem fitting in with other students, it took every ounce of effort I had. At the end of a school day, I would return home, go to my room, lock the door, and berate myself for whatever had occurred at school that day:

- I wasn't smart enough.
- I wasn't nice enough.
- Had I spoken inappropriately? (I had difficulty knowing what to say and what not to say.)
- Had I hurt anyone's feelings?
- Had I done anything wrong?
- Had people been laughing at me or with me?
- Had I broken any rules? (This was huge because I was a consummate rule follower and reprimander of anyone who even considered breaking a rule.)

I would sit in my room, filled with guilt, anger, and shame, because I had no idea what I had done correctly or incorrectly at school that day. I wasn't able to take away from each interaction whether or not it had been successful. And then I would spend the rest of the evening wondering what I would do wrong the next day.

These were the underlying feelings of my childhood, adolescence, and adulthood, every bit of it building and compounding over the years, leading to anxiety, bouts of depression, and an extremely negative sense of self.

So, what is it that I wish parents knew about Autistic girls?

That we need to know we are Autistic.

I have met many who don't want to tell their kids because they don't want them to know they're different. Folks, let me make one thing very clear: *we know.*

And whether it is feeling that we are bad, or wrong, or messed up—*however we choose to characterize ourselves*—we know we are different and that we do not fit in. And maybe that is because we don't know where we belong. We're looking in the wrong places, trying to be what we think we're supposed to be or what society has told us we have to be, and coming up short every time. I have a thirteen-year-old daughter who knows she is Autistic, and she is proud of the fact. She recognizes the struggles and challenges, and understands her need for accommodations so that she can be successful. But at the same time, she knows her strengths and capabilities. She knows she has a different neurology and because of it she experiences the world differently than non-Autistic people.

I knew my daughter was Autistic by the time she was nine, and per her request she was formally diagnosed at age eleven. I am here to impress upon you that she knew she was different by the time she was probably four or five years old. She didn't play with other children, she didn't want to be held or touched unless it was by me, she made very little eye contact, had no interest in toys, and didn't engage in imaginary play. (At this point you can get out your "Autism Warning Signs" checklists and follow along.) The point is, I never had to hide anything from my daughter so that she wouldn't think she was different. She knew then, and in truth, she's always known. Just like I had. The difference is, once I realized she was Autistic, unlike my parents, I began to educate not just her but our entire family: grandparents, aunts, uncles, and cousins included. My goal was not to raise my daughter to be like her peers, but to raise her to be herself—*an Autistic person with a love and understanding of who she is*—and autism is a big part of that.

Something else I wish parents of Autistic girls knew is who the experts really are.

We want our daughters to grow up with a positive sense of self and confidence in themselves and their abilities. Our girls are Autistic and always will be. No amount of therapy or intervention will ever change that, not that I would want it to! I am an advocate for autism acceptance and a firm believer in the importance neurodiversity plays in our lives. There are copious amounts of information on autism out there and many highly trained professionals producing it. Read it if you like; knowledge is important. Once you've finished reading it, however, I urge you to read books, articles, blogs, poetry, and whatever else you can get your hands on authored by actual Autistic women. These people, these Autistic women, are the experts in growing up Autistic. A hundred degrees on the wall from top universities may make you an expert in the field of a *disorder*, but they will never make you an expert on *being* Autistic.

I wish I had grown up knowing I was Autistic. Once I realized I was, I desperately wish I had known there were so many Autistic people out there, so willing to share their personal experiences to help others. I didn't begin meeting these amazing women until about four years after learning I was Autistic. Once I began reading their work and meeting them online, it felt like I was home. For the first time in my life I belonged. What if I had grown up knowing other people like myself? This is another thing I wish parents of Autistic girls knew: it's important for us to know other Autistic people.

I hear a lot of parents wanting to separate their Autistic children from others of the same neurology. They're worried about their children not progressing or possibly becoming more Autistic. *I'm not even sure what that means.*

I believe the idea is that if you don't tell us of our neurology and you surround us with non-Autistic peers, we'll never know, and after a time we'll become just like them. And in my case, it did work. My mother wasn't trying to hide my neurology from me; she didn't know. But let me share with you, growing up and attending school and being surrounded by non-Autistic people absolutely worked for me. *I was able to pass!*

No one knew! I was Autistic and no one, not even me, had any idea. I passed as a non-Autistic person for thirty-seven years! Outwardly, my rewards for passing included being accepted in social circles, doing well in school, and having friends. Well done Me, right? Well . . . Now I would like to share with you what passing on the outside did to me on the inside.

My days were filled with:

- Exhaustion

- Insomnia

- Depression

- Anger

- Obsessive-compulsive disorder

- Chronic panic attacks (meltdowns)

- Migraines

- Stress

- Anxiety

- Self-inflicted psychological abuse

- Low self-esteem

- Paranoia

- Unhealthy relationships

- Distrust of most people because I didn't fully
  understand social interaction or social cues

- Emotional confusion

- Constant frustration due to misunderstanding
  social situations

And I never told anyone.

And no one, neither family nor friends, ever knew. It took years for me to begin to like myself and that only began after diagnosis. I spent my life up until that point berating and tearing myself down for not being good enough. Putting a name to what made me different and understanding what those differences meant for and about me changed my life. I cannot put into words what it felt like to understand for the first time in my life that . . . *nothing was wrong with me.*

And with the realization that I was Autistic came many other revelations. My thoughts, feelings, and perceptions were not wrong; they were just different. Just as my repetitive mannerisms—*squinting, spinning, counting*—weren't freakish; they were forms of stimming. And my sensory integration issues, discomfort with eye contact, frustration with social expectations, and preference to be alone weren't rude or inappropriate behaviors I had to hide. All of these things, and many more, were merely the characteristics of me. I learned that I wasn't *odd, freakish*, or *wrong*. I learned that I was Autistic. And that's something else I wish parents of Autistic girls knew:

Our daughters are not ill, diseased, damaged, or broken. They do not need to be fixed.

If you have been given that information by any source, no matter how reliable you think it might be, *that source is wrong*. Autism is not a sickness, nor is it a disease. It is a different neurology. Our daughters are capable, valuable human beings no matter the extent of supports and accommodations that are necessary, and they should be spoken to and treated as such.

Oh! One last thing I wish parents of Autistic girls knew: Autism is something that should be talked about openly, honestly, and positively.

As parents, we need to begin to empower our daughters at a young age. Autism isn't something to be whispered and kept from us for fear of our finding out. That merely propagates the fear and misunderstanding of autism and what it really is. And what it really is differs from person to person, so let me emphasize this: Our first impressions of autism begin at home.

With our loved ones, parents, siblings, extended family, and friends, and how they receive the information. Our expectation of these people should be high. These are the people who should be there with us, to support and help empower our daughters.

There is a great deal of talk about how we can help families of Autistic kids, and that's important; we all need support. However, this conversation needs to be secondary. First and foremost, the conversation should be with and about our daughters. Get educated. Get an idea of what an Autistic life can be like. And again, this is where I ask you to consider the amazing Autistic women out there who share their lives with you through their writing.

Our Autistic daughters deserve love, acceptance, and respect for who they are. Anything less is unacceptable.

24 Autism, Sensory Experiences, and Family Culture

Mallory Cruz

Once my sensory issues were considered, things just went better for me.

1. Sensory Issues

When I was a kid, my mother loved to dress me, but I hated everything she put me in. It's not that I hated the designs themselves. To this day, I acknowledge that my mom's fashion sense has always been great, while mine is absolute garbage. It was because everything she dressed me in did not touch me right. Clothes that constantly touched my skin were bothersome. I still remember the short shorts she dressed me in, in sixth grade. I didn't care that my skin was showing, but the hem of the shorts was constricting on my thighs, constantly irritating me. I only wore them once.

Eventually, she let me choose the outfits I wanted, which ended up being "boys'" cargo shorts and pants, and "boys'" shirts that were baggy on me. I was finally comfortable, and I was much happier. I wasn't concerned with style; I just wanted to get through my school day without constantly pulling on my clothes. This fixed that.

I played contact sports all my life and injured many opponents. I love exaggeratedly gory horror movies. I don't take any pain meds when I get my period. Suffice to say, I consider myself a tough person.

But if I smell any eggs at all, no matter how they're cooked, I'll quite literally be incapacitated. The smell is quite figuratively my kryptonite. I'm not exaggerating when I say the smell makes me sick to my stomach. There are foods I just can't eat because my throat refuses to allow them down (tomatoes are too slimy). This includes foods I like (flan). It took a while for my parents to realize that I wasn't just being a picky eater (for example, I wouldn't eat if different foods touched each other), but that I was incapable of eating certain foods.

My parents started warning me when they were making eggs, and they'd make other vegetables for me when they used tomatoes.

Once my sensory issues were considered, things just became better for me.

Before writing this piece, I had called my mom to ask her about when I began to speak during childhood. She had told me before that I had started speaking at around one-and-a-half to two years old, which is considered developmentally delayed, and I wanted to confirm that. But it turns out I had misheard her.

As a baby, I was making eye contact and babbling and was overall very visibly connected to people until I was two years old, and then suddenly I started speaking less and making far less eye contact. What could have happened?

When I was born, I had hip dysplasia, which means my legs didn't grow into my hips. To set them in place, I wore a hip brace for the first two years of my life. At two years old, it was deemed okay to remove the hip braces. That's about the time when I stopped talking as much and making eye contact.

As my mom was telling me this over the phone, she remarked, "Oh, actually, now that I say that out loud, I bet it was taking away the hip braces that caused that, like it was a constant source of sensory input—it probably kept you grounded—and that was gone then."

It might be jarring to hear (read) me say (write) the following, but such a change wasn't a bad thing. For one thing, I personally find that story hilarious: my parents took something away that was affixed to my lower body to correct my legs and hips, and it led me to stop talking and making eye contact. And, of course, no one would make that connection, which is why it took nearly thirty years to solve that mystery—though I choose to believe I was punishing everyone for taking away my hip braces. I *can* hold a petty grudge for a long time.

More importantly, it led to me being diagnosed with a developmental delay, which helped me get the resources I needed. But also, there was nothing wrong with me when I started doing that either. It sounds like while my parents weren't prepared, they were able to adapt to that situation. But the solution, had they figured it out, would have been a very simple one: find something similar to give me that input again.

Overall, I include this story not for you all to go buy hip braces for your kids, but to really see how much sensory input, or lack of good sensory input, can really affect how we're behaving and feeling. Removing a constant source of sensory input changed my behavior drastically.

2. Diagnostic Criteria

The diagnostic criteria for autism is based on little white boys. Because it's based on a specific race and gender, it isn't easily put into context of other cultures; we don't see how it looks in non-white kids. Therefore, it's hard to get girls and children of color diagnosed. A white boy and a Black girl, both autistic or neurotypical, will be two totally different people, as they'll be socialized and raised differently, yet we only focus on one manifestation of autism.

Of course, this kind of medical bias isn't new: for example, most well-known heart attack symptoms are based on what a heart attack looks like in a cis man even though the symptoms are different in cis women. And some medical students literally believe that Black people physiologically feel less pain than white people because their skin is tougher (for real, look it up).

These biases cause us to fail children of color who need support that a diagnosis can come with.

For example, I'm Puerto Rican. I can't dance. To my family, it may have looked like I just didn't like dancing. Truth is, clumsiness in autistic people is common, and I was always clumsy as a kid. I couldn't dance because I couldn't control my body, and it didn't help I had Erb's palsy in my right arm, which affected my balance. Or that at family parties, I loved merengue and salsa music, but I hated music playing loudly because I had misophonia and it hurt my ears.

I feel empathy for others so strongly, but I'm not always great at knowing how to help. My autistic Dominican nephew shows empathy similarly. And while it's okay to not be empathetic, the idea that all autistics can't empathize is widespread.

It doesn't help that the media continues to push one representation of what an autistic person is: straight white boys who are unempathetic, have no sense of humor, and are bad at social cues. And it's frustrating to constantly see media portray autism the same way. I'd love to see an autistic character who isn't white, straight, and a boy.

Most of the criteria feels arbitrary, too. My niece can't get diagnosed because, though the signs are clearly there, her school grades are great. And that's it! Good grades are keeping her from getting diagnosed.

And some beliefs are massively misinformed. Don't even get me started on the belief that autistic people aren't funny. Some of the funniest people I know are autistic. I'm known for running a comedy blog. My nephew and niece are funny, and they are great at roasting my ass when I die in video games.

My point is, use the "criteria" loosely, or you'll miss more obvious clues to your child's autism and consequential needs.

3. Socializing with Other Autistic Kids

One of the best things my mother ever did for me was bring me to a group for autistic kids to learn social skills. I remember that the adults running it were struggling to get us to do small talk. It's common for autistic people to not be able to do small talk well, and I am no exception.

We were sitting in silence when I brought up *Invader Zim*, a Nickelodeon show that was on in 2003. I was obsessed with this show, and I wanted to talk about it, so I did. It turned out that the other kids were also obsessed. To the delight of the adults, we were all talking about our favorite characters, episodes we really liked, and jokes we thought were funny. I remember the silent excitement from the adults, like they had made a breakthrough. However, when they tried to shift the conversation back to "normal" small talk, it went dead.

I know now it's because autistic people get to the point. We thrive in that kind of setting. Autistic people don't follow the social norms of how conversations go, so instead of following a "normal" flow of conversation, we just talk about what we want to. Even when we make friends with normies, it's nice to have a break from the expected conversation rules. Even now, my autistic friends and I jump straight to talking about our special interests: we'll talk about the puppetry of *Little Shop of Horrors*, Leiji Matsumoto's work, flags, *DND* mechanics, and *The Magnus Archives* in a single conversation.

And there are so many rules to conversations that allistic people have. The main one is maintaining eye contact. It supposedly shows you're listening to the other person. If you aren't maintaining it, you're clearly not listening. Or it means you're lying about something. Those implications never made sense to me. Ask me if I'm listening, confirm that I am, don't assume I'm not over arbitrary body language. And if I'm really honest, if I'm making direct eye contact, I'm actually probably staring at something on your face. You know, gotta fake it 'til you make it.

There are also the rules for switching a topic. I used to find myself in this area where I'd be considered weird for changing a topic when I want to, but I'm also weird for not going along with a conversation changing when I had something to say on a topic. The flow of conversation almost feels tacitly decided on.

Small talk to me is the worst expectation for social interactions. The irony of small talk is that autistics are hounded about how we don't show interest in other people in "proper" ways, but then we're also required to ask non-questions; somehow, to show my caring about you, I need to ask you how's the weather, even though we both were outside at some point, or "how are you?" with the specific intent of receiving an "I'm fine" whether that's true or not, because if I answer honestly and say "I could be better," I might be dragging that person into a conversation they don't actually want to have. All these rules exist, but they don't come together. Small talk isn't always bad, but I can't imagine having it with someone I don't know well or at all. I'm okay existing with other people in a space in silence. I feel like I do it solely to deflect any undeserved suspicion.

If you want to know what it feels like to navigate conversations like this, one of my favorite game series is called *Persona*. One of the major mechanics of the game is that you can interact with people in-game and improve your social standing with them, and doing so makes your character stronger. *However,* when you interact with these characters, there are moments when you have to make the right dialogue choices to make them like you more. Sometimes you'll have multiple choices that are very similar, and it feels like there's no difference between your choices, so you think it's unimportant, and then you find out that the question had a right answer. Or you'll have a few choice answers and you'll see an obviously bad thing to say to anyone, and so you avoid it, only to find out that, actually, that bad thing to say to a person was the right thing to say and you were supposed to choose it. It can be frustrating to want to do well in this game and not know what the right thing to say is. So how can this be my favorite game series if this is an important function that reflects real life? Because I'm a cheater and I just search the correct dialogue choices online.

I do occasionally find myself thinking back to that meet-up years ago, and I think about how we got straight to the point and that's when we were all enthusiastic. These specific rules for conversing hold us back, even though we're capable of conversing if we're allowed to go by our own rules.

I can easily say, "Let your autistic child speak how they want to whoever because that's who they are," but I know that won't help them socialize. I genuinely believe societal expectations for what constitutes a "proper" conversation should and needs to shift so all people, autistic or otherwise, aren't demonized for not doing everything perfectly if they weren't being purposely rude or mean.

However, that will not happen tomorrow. That being said, if your child were just able to interact with others who converse similarly, I feel like some stress would be lifted off of them. They won't have to worry about if the conversation was weird for once, or find out they weirded people out and ostracized themselves.

4. Stimming

Most of my stims are always calming and grounding. I might stroke my arm or my finger occasionally, but my main stim is doodling. Since middle school, I've always doodled on everything. It actually helps me focus better. Even my notes from college notebooks and notes from work meetings are covered in scribbles. Consequently, I've been spoken to at most jobs I've worked at as an adult for it, though most of my superiors have thankfully understood. Only a month before writing this, I had to explain to my manager why I was doodling during a meeting. I'm grateful that he was understanding about it being an autistic stim, though he was less understanding about me also saying "shit" twice during that same meeting.

I also have throat stims, which is when I quote funny lines (usually yelled) from YouTube videos and shows. It just feels good.

I'm over thirty. My grown ass can't stop, probably won't stop, and neither can your child—nor should they. I'm relatively "lucky" to have inconspicuous stims and even those get me noticed. Help normalize your child's more noticeable stims. It most likely makes them feel good. Unless it's actively harmful to them or someone else, let them stim and make damn sure other adults in their life respect it.

5. Gender and Sexuality

Oh, hey, did you know there's been studies that show there's a sizable overlap of autistic individuals who are also trans/non-binary in some way. I can tell you that it's probably because if you have a spectrum disorder, where you're not concerned with social norms, you probably won't care about the gender norms pushed on everyone, so it's easier to explore your gender.

I personally forgot I had a gender back in the mid-2010s, and I haven't been bothered to care about it since.

It's also funny to me that everyone thought I was gay because of how I dressed in middle and high school, but my clothes were never related to my sexuality. I wasn't gay because of how I dressed, because I'm not gay. I'm bi because of my attraction to men, women, and nonbinary people.

Basically, please be open to any of your kids not being heterosexual and/or cisgender.

As I stated earlier, my biggest concern was comfort. I was not always concerned with how others perceived me. The best way to describe my own personal experience in how I navigated my own sexuality is that I actively didn't do so. I experienced and decided things as they happened. Until my senior year, I thought I was just straight. I was attracted to boys. I wouldn't realize otherwise until my senior year of high school, and while I had crushes throughout high school, they weren't my priority. I wasn't concerned with dating until college. In high school, how I dressed or looked to others was not affected by this. Not that I dressed ugly; my mom made sure that if I dressed in boys' clothes, that the outfit looked good.

It's hard to explain, but the idea that these two things could affect one another, that how I dressed and my dating life might influence the other, never occurred to me. It wasn't quite a direct thought that the person I liked should accept me for who I am so much as it never occurred to me. After all, I did have a boyfriend during high school, and later in life, I realized there were boys who were interested in me (though I wasn't aware they were dropping hints of such since I couldn't read those cues). And when I eventually realized I was bi, I didn't panic. I remember thinking, *Oh, okay, you're bi now*, and expanded who I sought out. Dating's not easy for the obvious autistic reasons, but at least I'm not struggling to figure out what I'm looking for, and that has made the absolute nightmare that is modern dating much easier.

But all these things came together for me because I was allowed to explore them how I wanted. I was able to see what kind of partner I wanted no matter their gender because I was allowed to think for myself and didn't concern myself with what society said I should want. I can't say that I'm completely immune to what society pushes me to find attractive or what I should have in a partner, or how I should be putting myself out there for others to see, but I'm fully aware of when that's happening. I'm fully aware of how I feel about people. In my eyes, your role as a parent in regard to dating is to observe, and advice is helpful if it's sought out, but don't be condescending or think that you know what is best for everyone as if there's one answer. Letting us navigate our sexuality and gender and how we want to express it until we come for advice is beneficial for us. Society pushes a heteronormative ideal for all of us, so whether your child is cis and hetero, or figures out they're trans or bi or gay or a lesbian or whatever else, we're gonna catch crap if we're not 100 percent following heteronormativity perfectly. The least you can do is not add to it.

6. Overall, just be open-minded.
Roll with everything.
Consider what may be social constructs.

When you just roll with things and keep an open mind, it's easier to see how certain expectations you have are just social constructs. When you challenge why certain manifestations of autism bother you, you'll see that it's society's rigidity for how we should act and behave that's the issue.

25 Safe Harbors in a Difficult World

Kayla Rodriguez

It seems like the world is against autism, and I'm here to tell you that it's not right.

WHEN I LOOK BACK on my childhood, I often remember how difficult it was. Being autistic didn't make it difficult, it was society's reaction to autism that often made it unbearable. I grew up during a time when I thought it was rare to be autistic because not only was I the only autistic girl I knew, but I was the only autistic I knew in general. Now I realize that being autistic wasn't rare, but that people weren't diagnosed as autistic until later in life, which is unfortunately common, especially in girls and women. Women and other genders weren't being diagnosed because most autism research was centered around boys and men.

Though diagnoses are on the rise, society's opinion of autism hasn't really changed. While people are not publicly trying to "cure" autism anymore, a lot of autism organizations, including Autism Speaks, still try to "prevent" and "treat" autism as if it's some terrible disease. Parents often try to "cure" their autistic children by harmful means that will never work, like drinking bleach. The puzzle piece that is present in most of the logos of autism organizations, including the famous one by Autism Speaks, is viewed by many autistics to symbolize that autistic people are missing something. Then there's applied behavioral analysis, or ABA, which is a harmful "therapy" that most people recommend for young autistics, especially autistic children. There is also the high chance that autistic children can be bullied in school and called the R-word and other hurtful things, much like I was throughout school.

My mother fought and advocated for me throughout school and helped me as I was bullied. However, not every autistic child is so lucky to have supportive and accepting parents. Some parents of autistic children even kill them because of their autism. This is why various disability organizations take part in the annual Disability Day of Mourning, to remember those we lost this way.

There's also the anti-vaccination movement in which people believe that vaccines cause autism, even though this theory was proven false long ago. These people refuse to vaccinate their children and sometimes let their children get sick or die rather than get them the recommended immunizations, because in their minds, being diagnosed as autistic is worse than death.

It seems like the world is against autism, and I'm here to tell you that it's not right. Autism isn't a bad "disease" that needs to be "cured" or "prevented," and it isn't worse than death. Vaccines don't cause autism and autistic people aren't missing anything. Autistic people are whole, and we are people with feelings and thoughts just like everyone else. All autistics have a voice, even though some might express it differently (either through a device if they are nonverbal or their social skill differences). We can find love and have children and be successful in life; we just need support and accommodations to accomplish those things. We do deserve to live a fulfilling life. That's the first thing I want every parent of an autistic child to know. The second thing is please don't ever hurt, abuse, or kill your autistic child. There is always a better solution to the temporary stress you're experiencing while raising your autistic child.

The third thing is to make sure you're supporting a good organization that helps, supports, and advocates for autistics. Make sure their logo doesn't have a puzzle piece on it and if they have a logo like the infinity logo. This is because many autistics don't like the puzzle piece. Many autistics, including myself, see the puzzle piece like autistics are missing something crucial when we're not. Many autism organizations have that puzzle piece logo, and they try to "cure," "prevent," or "treat" autism. You should avoid donating to and/or supporting these organizations entirely. The ideal autism organization you should support or donate to shouldn't support ABA and they should actually advocate for autistics, like by hosting Disability Day of Mourning or letting autistics know of good opportunities for employment, socializing, etc. They should have helpful resources to learn more about autism in a positive way and social groups to make sure your child isn't alone. They should not try to "cure," "prevent," or "treat" autism. They should try instead to help and support autistics all throughout their lives, from childhood to adulthood, and promote and advocate for the rights of autistic people and autism acceptance—not awareness. For the most part, people are now aware of autism, but they don't accept it. A great autism organization should be promoting acceptance, in addition to doing the things I've mentioned before.

Parents, please listen to your child because they know themselves best and how they need to be supported by you. Try to make sure that your child gets the support and accommodations they need when they're young. You can try Family Support or Home- and Community-Based Services Medicaid waivers. If your autistic child wants to be social, research programs or meetups that they can be a part of. If they're nonverbal, make sure you get them an assistive communication device to help them express their voice. Get them noise-cancelling headphones if they're sensitive to loud noise. You should look up alternatives to ABA so that your autistic child won't be harmed when getting help.

Autistics can go to college and succeed, but if they're not interested, please accept and support that. Employment is difficult for autistics, and a lot of autistics are unemployed. Help them find a job through employment services. Teach them the essentials in life and don't assume they can't live on their own because with help they can. Go to a Center for Independent Living for help if/when they want to live on their own. However, the most important thing is to *listen* to your child and ensure that *they* are the ones who get to decide what they want or what they need; it's your job to help them get there. And while it's important to advocate for them, make sure you teach them to advocate for themselves, as well. My mother was my advocate in my youth. Eventually, as I grew into adulthood, I learned to advocate for myself. Your child should do the same for accommodations at school, work, and other areas in their life.

Another thing I want to impart to parents of autistic children is that when your child gets diagnosed as autistic, don't make assumptions about them. People often make assumptions and stereotype autistics because of how autism is portrayed in mainstream media. When autism is portrayed in the media, which is rare, it is mostly false, negative, and inaccurate. Not every autistic is "gifted" and proficient in technology and/or math and science. Not every autistic is like Sheldon Cooper or the protagonists of *The Good Doctor* and *Atypical*.

The autistic community isn't made up of only cisgender, asexual, straight, white male geniuses that TV shows tend to portray. Also, not every autistic is an introvert. Some autistics, like me, are extroverts and love being around people. Not every autistic bangs their head on the wall or flaps their hands and are nonverbal. As a Puerto Rican autistic lesbian, I didn't see anyone like me on TV or in the movies growing up, so I felt alone. Part of that was due to the lack of representation in the media. Try to show them positive examples of representation like Pixar's *Loop* on Disney+ and the TV show *Everything's Gonna Be Okay*. You should tell your child that they are never alone and look for examples of positive autistic representation that you can introduce them to. Remember that when you meet an autistic, you've only met *one* autistic. That means that some autistics may do similar things and have similar interests, but we are all different, just like everyone else.

Parents of autisic children should know that autistics can be a part of many different communities, including the disability community, the BIPOC (Black, Indigenous, and People of Color) community, and the LGBTQIA+ community. Being part of these marginalized and oppressed communities means autistics will deal with what neurotypical (aka non-autistic) people in these communities go through, but because they're autistic, they will deal with it in their own unique way. Autistics can also have mental illness and be suicidal. Please make sure you support them through all this, and if they're mentally ill, make sure they get the help they need. I know from experience, as a member of these communities and being mentally ill, that these communities can be ableist (they discriminate against people with disabilities), which makes it hard for autistics to find their place in them. Also be careful when it comes to law enforcement. From my experience, the police can misunderstand autistics in an emergency situation, and it can be deadly for us. Unfortunately, parents have to teach their autistic children how to act when police are around, especially if their child is BIPOC. Finally, be careful when it comes to language. Don't use "severe" or the functioning labels. Use what your child and the autistic community prefers.

It's so hard for autistics to live in a world that doesn't accept us. Please be a safe haven for your child. Listen to them, support them, and guide them so they can live a happy and fulfilling life.

26 Give Your Daughters Autistic Community

Jean Winegardner

There is so much that autistic women and girls can give to each other.

▬▬▬▬

I THINK THE HARDEST PART of growing up as an undiagnosed autistic woman was the aloneness. This is different than loneliness. I have been fortunate to have friends for most of my life, but with few exceptions, I have felt apart from them.

I spend a lot of time alone in my head and until I got my autism diagnosis at age thirty-eight and started to better understand my neurology, much of that time in my head was spent wondering why I felt out of step with a lot of people. Because I didn't know any autistic people nor did I know the many ways to be autistic, I assumed that the fault in my different steps lay with me.

When I was eight and my teacher asked the class what humans need to survive, instead of saying food, shelter, or clothing, I said the sun. I believed her when she told me I was wrong, because she couldn't see the truth in a more literal answer than she was prepared for.

When I was eighteen and suddenly realized that people made eye contact a lot, I trained myself to look people in the eye all the time without realizing that it was okay not to.

When I was twenty-three and people made fun of me for not liking to be hugged, I believed that there was something defective about me for not wanting to embrace my family.

When I was twenty-eight and my neighbors down the street played music outside their apartment, which no one in my house could hear but that drove me out of the house because I couldn't tolerate listening to the nearly inaudible bass thumping, I assumed that I was intolerant instead of understanding that I had sensory differences.

Had I had an autistic community during those times, I might have realized that other people saw the world the way I did, that there were other people who weren't huggers or eye-lookers, that my brain interpreted sensory input in a way that made some of it intolerable to me. Had I had an autistic community then, I could have helped someone else with that knowledge as well.

I worked as hard as I could to build a life full of love and support and friends, and I have done a pretty good job. I earned a master's degree, I have lived on my own, I got married, and I had kids. I have held several good jobs, even though staying at one place of employment for longer than a couple of years has been hard.

By the time I'd lived in my current home outside of Washington, DC, for a few years, I had built a wonderful community, one that I still love, but I had built a neurotypical community, something that has become harder and harder to be at total peace with as I have come to embrace my own neurodivergence.

If I think of one thing I lack, one thing that could have made my life easier from the time I was a child up until recent days, it would be being a part of an autistic community. It is something that has been noticeably lacking from much of my life, and it is something I crave.

I am raising two autistic sons, one of whom was diagnosed five years before I was. He was in a full inclusion classroom up to and through third grade. He has friends who are neurotypical. Through his association with his siblings and their friends, he hangs out with a lot of non-autistic people.

Yet, even with so many people who love and accept him, those that he is happiest and most relaxed around are from his autistic community. He is fortunate to have a large autistic and non-neurotypical community. He is in a partially self-contained classroom with several other autistic kids. His two best friends are on the spectrum. He played hockey on a special hockey team where no one judges him for being unabashedly himself. He meets autistic adults when I take him out to community events.

My son may feel sad and worried and alone sometimes, but it won't be because he thinks that he is the only one who thinks literally or because he is the only one he knows who scripts to communicate. He will grow up knowing that echolalia is how lots of people communicate and that doing it with a friend who loves it too can be one of the best ways to spend an afternoon. He will grow up with the knowledge that using a fidget feels great and is totally okay. He will grow up knowing that being autistic is a wonderful way to be.

He will grow up knowing that he is not alone.

I can't fault my family for any of my isolation. They were and are loving and wonderful and they gave me a lovely childhood. I am very lucky. Women my age and with my neurological makeup weren't given diagnoses when we were kids. Now that I am an adult, the responsibility for finding community rests with me, something that has become easier with online social media, but which is still so very difficult for me due to my social anxiety.

My wish for young autistic people is that their parents listen to them and facilitate friendships with whomever they want to hang out with. But I think it is so important that these kids are given opportunities to build relationships with other autistic kids.

There is so much that autistic women and girls can give to each other, including love, laughter, joy, kind smiles, critical thought, understanding, and true safety. Instead of striving to conform to a neurotypical norm, these friendships can let our young women be who they are on their own terms. Navigating the complicated social rules of girls and women is so very difficult. Doing it with a friend or two who truly understand and like you for who you are makes it, if not easier, at least less painful.

I watch my son when he settles into his familiar groove with his best friend, who is also autistic. They fall into step and walk in circles around our house or our yard and talk in their easy rhythm. Some of it is scripted and has been since they met each other more than a decade ago in kindergarten. More of it is spontaneous now, but all of it is easy and happy and filled with total acceptance.

There is so much pressure on parents of autistic kids to encourage them to be friends with typical kids. I am all for that. I believe that we all have things to learn and to enjoy about each other, regardless of neurostatus. That said, finding your tribe is a powerful thing. Autistic peers and older role models can do so much to help younger kids with their self-esteem, self-awareness, and feelings of safety.

I still struggle with finding autistic community, but what I have found has helped me so very much.

Now when I have meltdowns, I understand what they are and how to ride them out without mentally punishing myself or thinking I am being irrational. When I can't tolerate the touch of someone's hand on me, I know that it isn't anyone's fault and that it is okay to move away. When my answer to a question is off because I interpreted it differently than it was meant, I can laugh at myself and know that I'm not wrong.

Furthermore, when I get questioning looks because I'm not holding up my end of the conversation as expected or when my thought process can't quite catch up to the questions I'm being asked, I know that the fault isn't with me.

I know these things—and so many more—because I have found autistic community and the knowledge and support that come with it—and this makes me less alone.

27 A Parents' Guide to Being Transgender and Autistic

Alexandra Forshaw

Trying to fit in has been a life-long undertaking, as much a consequence of being autistic as of being transgender.

▬▬▬▬▬

TRANSGENDER PEOPLE are now more widely recognized than ever. A major UK soap opera had a transgender regular character for sixteen years. A Manhattan-based chain of luxury department stores used transgender models in an ad campaign for spring 2014. A transgender actress was featured on the cover of *Time* magazine in May 2014. But despite this, most people still know little if anything about us. Reliable estimates put the incidence of gender dysphoria —discomfort with one's assigned gender—at about one in five hundred.[1] However, there is evidence from some small studies that the rate may be as much as eight times higher among autistic people.[2]

As a child, I didn't know anything about it. I was born forty years ago and labeled as a boy based on external appearances. Growing up in an environment that was entirely populated with white, heterosexual people, there was no way for me to gain experience of anything outside of that. There was no internet, only the books at home and at school, which I read voraciously. But these books presented a similar picture of the world to the limited view I had from the small English village where I lived. A completely binary view: people divided into men and women.

The trouble was that not knowing anything about transgender people or gender dysphoria didn't change the fact that I knew I wasn't comfortable being a boy. From the age of about ten I would borrow my mother's clothes on occasion. I felt more comfortable dressing as a girl, as if I was being my natural self. I always thought my mother didn't suspect because she never mentioned anything to me. To be fair, she knew nothing about gender dysphoria, and conversations on the subject of sexual or gender matters just didn't happen in our family.

It would be true to say that I would not have ever felt comfortable talking to my parents about being female. For all I knew I was the only person in the whole world who felt that way. It was all so far outside my experiences that I would not have been able to explain anything properly. But more than that, there was my assumption that my feelings were wrong, unnatural, that I had to keep them hidden or else I might face censure or punishment—all a result of topics like this never being talked about at home.

Trying to fit in has been a life-long undertaking, as much a consequence of being autistic as of being transgender. Like most autistic people of my generation, I was not diagnosed during childhood; I was just seen as preternaturally shy, a loner more likely to be seen with my head in a book than playing with others. My social awkwardness made me a target for bullying—name calling and occasional threats rather than physical violence. The last thing I was going to contemplate was providing more ammunition by telling anybody that I believed I was a girl.

I lived that life, keeping my secret to myself, for about thirty years. Several years ago, I discovered, after following up on an initial suggestion made by my wife, that I am autistic. To call this a revelation would be a considerable understatement. Suddenly, so much of my life up to that point came into focus. I understood why I am the way I am and why I struggle with certain aspects of life. I became more introspective and analytical about my own behavior, studying myself, reading about autism, and applying what I learned to gain a deeper insight into myself.

One effect of this was that I also started to research transgender experience and gender dysphoria. At last I had the vocabulary to describe what I had known for so long. I was still too afraid to tell anybody else about it, but I began to drop hints into conversation.

Not that anybody picked up on them: people tend to dismiss such small clues because they do not fit their expectations.

In the end, my hand was forced. Hiding my real self for so long had taken its toll on me and I descended into a lengthy bout of depression, primarily caused by my gender dysphoria. I was unable to work for several weeks, and my relationship with my wife deteriorated almost to the point of breaking up. To have the chance to regain some happiness in my life and become fit to work again, I came out and admitted that I was a transgender woman, and I started the long process of transition to bring my body in line with my self-image. It was as if a weight had been lifted from me, and at long last I feel happy. I am free to be myself.

Looking back, I have regrets. There are things I wish had been different. I wish I had known something about the spectrum of gender identities and expressions. I wish I had felt comfortable enough to speak to my parents about how I felt. I wish they had the knowledge and experience to understand gender issues.

Some children identify as a different gender from an early age, even as soon as they are able to communicate. In some cases, especially for autistic children, they may not have a strong sense of their own gender and want to fit in with a particular group of other children. Until your child can tell you unequivocally how they feel, there is no way to tell for sure whether your daughter is a tomboy or a boy. Like one's sexual orientation, being transgender is not a choice. It is simply the way a person is. The most important thing is that your child has no doubts that you, their parent, will love and accept them regardless. It's about honesty and openness.

Talking about gender with your child is very important. When they see a transgender person on TV, this would be an ideal time to introduce the subject. You could explain how some people look like a woman (or a man) but are really the opposite gender. Their minds tell them that they are a man, but their bodies look like they are a woman's and that makes them feel unhappy. For some, just dressing as a man and looking like a man is enough to make them happy, but others will need the help of doctors to change their bodies. Having role models helps a lot by demonstrating that there are other people out there who have gone through something similar: people like Cher's son, Chaz Bono; directors of *The Matrix*, Lana Wachowski and Lilly Wachowski; actor and writer Scott Turner Schofield; lead singer of punk band *Against Me!*, Laura Jane Grace; and computer scientist and engineer Lynn Conway.

Over time, if your child consistently insists that she is a boy, perhaps even insisting for years, then that is a sign that she may be transgender. The reality is that while a lot of children simply go through phases, there is a significant minority who do not conform to their assigned gender over the long term. Whatever the signs, until your child is able to tell you for themselves, you cannot know for sure. The best approach for your child's wellbeing is to be approachable and accepting, not critical. They will need love and support, because on top of her differences through being autistic, they will face discrimination and prejudice for not conforming according to their gender. Denying how they feel and not believing them will only cause them distress.

Your support can start with small things such as allowing her to dress as a boy at home, to have a boyish haircut, to play with toys that you might consider more appropriate for boys. None of this is going to change whether your child identifies as a girl, a boy, or something in between in the long run, but it will affect their happiness in the here and now. It may turn out that this is just a phase of growing up, and they later decide that they feel like a girl. But in some cases, it is not a phase and the feelings persist.

As parents, it is likely that you will find dealing with this difficult. It's common to feel nervous, worried, embarrassed, or even angry. Some parents feel grief at the "loss" of their daughter when she becomes their son. There are parallels here with the feelings parents experience when their child is diagnosed with autism: There may be shock and denial at first and fear because you do not understand what is happening. Your expectations have turned out to be at odds with reality. Receiving any kind of unanticipated news is enough to knock most people off balance, and all the more so when it involves someone as close to you as your child.

It takes time for the new information to sink in, but don't lose sight of this key fact: The only thing that is different right now is that you have a piece of information about your child that you didn't possess yesterday. Your child has not changed at all. They were the same person before you received this news and continue to be the same person now.

You will almost certainly encounter conflict with other people who do not understand, such as other parents at your child's school. Keep in mind that whatever other people may think or say, it is your child's happiness that is most important. Discuss things with your child's school; enlist the support of the teaching staff and classroom assistants who are responsible for your child while she is there. Encourage the school to involve other parents, to inform them about your child's situation and the challenges she faces. Other children will be influenced by their parents, which is why it is important to involve them in the process.

Nothing you did as parents caused this; it is simply the way your child is. It is not a blessing, but neither is it a curse. Nothing you do now or in the future will change your child's gender identification. What you can affect, though, is how happy your child is. I keep going on about support because that really is the most important thing. Providing a parent's unconditional love to your child, accepting them for whoever they may be, and making that explicitly clear throughout their life will make the world of difference to their happiness.

28 On Surviving Loneliness and Isolation, and Learning to Live with Loss

Lydia X. Z. Brown

I understand now that I've lived my life as the person in-between.

I'M WRITING THIS to my mom and dad, full of hope and dreams and sorrow and grief and appreciation for who I was when I still lived at home, when I was growing up in your house.

You must have remembered how lonely and friendless I often felt. How I struggled with bullies at school, with students and teachers both in on it sometimes. I can't remember a time when I felt like I truly belonged anywhere. In years of talking to other autistic people, hundreds of other autistic people, this sense of constant alienation, isolation, separation, and loneliness turns out to be incredibly common.

Most clinicians and so-called autism professionals would say that this is because we as autistic people lack social skills and suffer from impairments in social reciprocity, empathy, and social skills. But you knew me—and you knew how I was terrified of making my friends upset or angry at me, and how I wanted nothing more than to make sure they felt happy.

What you might not have known is that I was terrified of losing all the friends I had. Fifth grade was one of the best years I had had because it was the only year when I felt like I had a group of friends in school who cared about me and were friends with each other. It turned out, of course, that many of the people in that group weren't actually my friends—or even friends with each other.

And even at a young age, other kids knew: one of the best ways to get me to do something funny for other kids to laugh at was to convince me to do something meant to be socially awkward or wrong or deviant somehow, banking on the combination of my social obliviousness and my desire to please others to see it all through. Like the time other kids told me to tell a girl that I thought she was hot—a word that I thought just meant pretty (but had intuitively sensed that it probably meant something else, too). The joke, of course, was that I liked girls, and since I was supposed to be a girl, that meant I was doing something wrong.

But liking boys didn't work out either. There were the years when I hung out with a boy known to be in special ed classes, the kid that everyone else called a retard. You told me that it would be bad if I let people take pictures of me because someone might make a fake picture showing my face on someone else's body with a boy. Someone did, in fact, do that. And the fact that that boy and I danced together at a class dance made us both fodder for jokes meant to mock the fact that we were both weirdos and retards—bullying that didn't even make much sense, because I was also constantly made fun of for being interested in books and being a nerd.

Since childhood, I've learned that many autistic people form much closer relationships and friendships with people significantly older or younger than we are, which is incredibly noticeable as a child, where spending time with kids two grades older or younger, or with the teachers, is an excellent way to be marked a weirdo right away. As adults, it can take different forms—friendships with people in different stages of life than our own, regardless of exact ages.

For me, the circumstances of my life have undoubtedly shaped the specific type of loneliness and alienation I continue to feel in adulthood. I knew from a young age that I was different from my peers—for better and worse. I always knew. I didn't always use the same words or language to describe myself as I do now, nor did I know all the things I do now. But as a Chinese kid with white parents, and a sister who is also Chinese but clearly of a different ethnicity than me, I already knew that I did not belong. No matter what you wanted for me—to love and be loved, to be raised to be kind and also just, smart and also humble, giving and also careful—there was no escaping the racial dynamics of the kind of transracial and transnational adoption my sister and I became subjects of.

It's impossible for white adoptive parents of children of color to ever fully understand the political, social, and cultural dynamics surrounding transracial and transnational adoption, including the adoption industry's deep connections to white supremacy, settler colonialism, and family separation. Most adoptive parents—even if we're limiting this to the pool of adoptive parents who actually mean well, and exclude the ones adopting for consciously predatory or exploitative reasons—want the best for the children they choose to bring home. But there are also layers to the ableism we have to deal with when the adopted children turn out disabled.

You remember when the school psychologist decided—in contrast to the neuropsychologist you'd taken me to—that I couldn't possibly be autistic, but instead must have reactive attachment disorder because of the trauma caused by adoption and my early weeks or months (or however long it really was) in a state-operated orphanage? (Ironically, given my current work as a disability rights and disability justice advocate, another kind of institution lesser-named in disability work.) You might not have known that that specific diagnosis is a way to stigmatize people who've survived trauma in early childhood, especially trauma caused by family relations or family separation—and it's often coded by race and class too.

I know that I'm autistic, and I know that like most other autistic people, I've survived trauma after trauma throughout my life. Some of that trauma is what we call ordinary trauma—things that might seem small or minor to people outside our lives, but that nonetheless affects us profoundly. Much of the trauma I've experienced, both in childhood and adulthood, has been connected to isolation and the loss of friends. Social ostracism and shunning are dangerous and deeply violent, whether done within a family unit, in school, in a religious cult, or in an identity-based community.

I don't think you could have predicted that. But I wish you had known just how much it hurt to be told that I had friends and people who loved me, because in moments when I was grieving the loss of friends, or the realization that people I'd thought were friends were actually bullies or abusers, what I actually needed to hear was simply an affirmation that what I was experiencing was awful. That sometimes people are terrible. That sometimes it's not meant to work out. That sometimes life brings awful bitterness and sorrow, and the only correct reactions are grief and rage.

Even today, I still gravitate toward other loners. Anywhere I go, I have an intuitive sense for the weird and lonely people, often other disabled, sick, mad, neurodivergent, queer, and trans people. We witness each other. We know each other. We can recognize other people who share this pain. The pain of constant rejection and fear of rejection. The pain of trying our damndest to be kind and decent people only to be exploited and betrayed over and over again, often with little or no explanation. This happens to autistic people on such a stunning scale that there probably should be specific research done on it, though I suspect that some of the reason this is so common for us is that many of us can be overly trusting and wish the best for others, even if we are at the same time deeply distrustful and wary of them because of the trauma we've survived. We are often deeply principled and wedded to the values we grow up with and the values we adopt later in life, and as a result, many of us are deeply concerned with a sense of fairness or justice. That instinct means that we're often well-placed to support others like us—and in exactly the right position to be ridiculed by peers, isolated within our social networks, or targeted for manipulation by people seeking to exploit us.

I wish you'd taught me better how to set and enforce boundaries for myself—for my time, my energy, my space, my life, and my love. You wanted me to be safe—most parents who are at least even halfway decent want this for their children. I would give anything for my younger self to have been able to feel both safe and free at the same time.

I understand now that I've always lived my life as the person in-between. I've struggled for years to make sense of my queer and trans identity and experiences, as an asexual person often assumed (incorrectly) to be a woman, who's been at times femme and at times masculine of center, and who's been in heterosexual as well as queer relationships. I've spent years developing a clear and specific understanding of my own positionality as an East Asian person of color and what that means in both how I experience privilege in society and specific racist oppression. In disability advocacy, we're often stuck between being called not disabled enough to have a say on disability or too disabled to be able to have a say on anything at all. That kind of in-betweenness for me has never been limited only to my social and political identities, though, and marks every aspect of my life.

You remember how I usually had friends outside school but not as much in school? How my friends were often in different grades? How I left your church's youth group because of the extreme alienation I felt from the other youth and the pastor alike? How I decided to leave activity after activity? I don't remember what I had said at the time as to why, but I remember now that I never felt like I belonged, was good enough to stay, or would be able to stay for too long before others would decide that I didn't belong. I was always the odd one out—and never able to feel comfortable for long. Even in my fiction and roleplay writing, I'm struck by the shared *loneliness* among my characters.

Research and personal accounts have documented that autistic people are significantly more likely to be victimized by bullying and abuse of all types throughout our lives. You once told me how hurt you felt whenever you learned that someone had been mean to me. As an adult, I understand and appreciate this sentiment—a type of offering of compassion or empathy. As a child, what I needed to hear, what I wish other autistic, neurodivergent, mad, sick, and disabled children could know, is how much our parents cared that *we* were hurting.

I've thrived as an adult in many ways. I have friends and a partner, and in many ways, fulfilling passions and work (to the extent that we can be happy about the work we do). But the persistent sense of alienation and loneliness has never left. Nor has the fear of losing friends. More than anything else, I wish that parents of autistic children would understand that we don't need people to speak *for* us, or even to keep us safe in a world that is fundamentally unsafe, so much as we need our parents to demonstrate what it's like to develop healthy friendships. Positive family relationships, romantic relationships, and collegial relationships all have in common the basic tenets of a good friendship: trust, care, respect, and mutuality. I don't miss the complex drama of the middle school years, and I certainly don't want to re-experience the traumas that have shaped my life since then. But I do remember well the ways in which you showed me that love across identities and experiences is possible—in making sure I could take Chinese language classes at a Chinese cultural center, in writing notes back and forth while in-character as part of my imaginary world, in encouraging me to explore all the things I loved to do, on my terms, in my way.

You were not perfect, and neither was I.

I have become a person that I hope my younger self would be proud to know and perhaps look up to. And I have brought the full weight of my grief, my losses, my traumas, and my hard-fought, hard-won growth with me into a world where I know I may never belong by others' standards, but where I'll make damn sure I never stop fighting until we can all experience love and rest and community and care, past isolation, past survival.

29 There's a Place

Emily Paige Ballou

I want you to know that your child is a whole person, just as they are.

I WANT YOU TO KNOW that there is a place in the world for your child.

I want you to know that whether or not she grows up to have a "normal" life isn't the most important thing.

I want you to know that there is no shortage of wonder and of rewarding experiences in the world, even if his life doesn't resemble the one you might've anticipated for him.

I want you to know that she can have a life that works for her.

Even if she never speaks.

Even if she never looks you in the eye.

Even if he doesn't go to prom.

Even if she never goes to college.

Even if he's never able to drive.

Even if she never has a romantic partner or gets married.

Even if she never has children of her own.

Even if it takes them much longer to learn things that are easy for other people.

Even if she will never be able to live independently or will always need help and support with daily living skills.

Even if she self-injures.

Even if she might not be able to work at a conventional job. Even if she needs to take advantage of disability or Social Security benefits.

Even if she is gender nonconforming.

Even if she can't wear makeup or dress the way that a lot of people think girls should because of sensory issues.

Even if she has trouble with hygiene or self-care right now.

Even if her comfort zone seems very narrow or restricted right now.

Even if some or all of these things are true and remain true, there is a place in the world for your child, because the world is so big, so wide, and so diverse. I want you to know that there are autistic people who fit all of these descriptions, living lives that they're okay with and find worthwhile, because there are an indefinite number of ways to make a good life, not just the one that we're often led to believe is the only way. I want you to know that people who fit all of those descriptions do things like have friends, have hobbies, have passionate interests, take online courses if they don't go to college, write and blog, engage in advocacy, volunteer, work, enjoy the natural world, and are loved and appreciated.

I want you to know that your child's finding her place in the world doesn't depend on how well she pretends to be what other people want or expect her to be, but on finding the places where other people are most okay with who she actually is. I want you to know that those places are multiplying.

I want you to know that your child has real, innate strengths and not just splinter skills or savant skills, as many people assume are the only kinds of talents that autistic people might have. Some of them may be intrinsically related to her being autistic, and some may not, but your child has strengths, and figuring out what they are and nurturing them will help her find that place in the world.

They might be things like pattern recognition, attention to detail, complex visualization, instinct for math or music, rhythm and cadence, dance, movement, empathy and compassion, a strong sense of justice and fairness, the tendency to see an issue or a problem from a different perspective, memory, intuition, sensitivity to her environment, a high tolerance or even relish for repetition, ritualization, or solitude, resistance to boredom, having a rich and detailed internal life, working with her hands, mechanical understanding, working easily with plants or animals, pragmatic problem solving, spiritual insight, poetry, and metaphor . . .

And they might be in a way of understanding the world that I can't even name or conceive of.

I want you to know that your child has strengths to nurture even if they also have immense challenges. Even if you can't see what they are yet. Even if your child doesn't know what they are yet. Even if he can't show them or communicate them to you yet. Even if the professionals and therapists and educators in your lives have only told you all about your child's deficits and challenges.

And although some kinds of therapy might help her, she will need time and opportunity to indulge and develop her desires and strengths, not only to remediate her deficits. It is very likely that where she'll demonstrate her best skill development, or learn the most about how she works and what she's good at, won't be in any therapy or in any classroom, but in some way just by doing what she loves in the world.

I want you to know that what he might never do doesn't necessarily tell you anything about what he might do.

I want you to know that your child is a whole person, just as they are. That she is not lacking any essential feature of what it means to be human. There is no missing piece of her you have to find; she is all there, even if you don't know how to understand her yet. I want you to know that he does have an intact mind. It's just a mind that may work very differently from those of the people around him, in ways that are still obscure to most of us, in ways that he doesn't know how to tell you about yet.

I want you to know that she has a future as an autistic person.

I want you to know that your child is of value to the world, and the world has a place and a need for them.

Conclusion

Beth Ryan

Your autistic daughter needs you to embrace all of the wonderful possibilities of her selfhood.

YEARS WENT BY before my daughter was diagnosed with autism. During those years, she underwent a multitude of tests for various diseases that would inevitably result in pain, suffering, and death. Although it was delivered to us as though it were bad news, the autism diagnosis was a relief. I immediately began searching the internet and was mostly directed to sites like Autism Speaks, where I learned what a horror it was to have an autistic child. So, I stopped searching because my child was nothing like the children I was reading about, although the autism "specialist" at her school described her in similar terms to the tragic poster children. I couldn't distance myself from what I read fast enough.

It is not socially acceptable to embrace a child's disability as a beautiful part of her selfhood—to not wish for some non-disabled version of that child. Instead of following your natural parental instinct to love, nurture, and protect your child, you are compelled in no uncertain terms to become a behavioral compliance officer of sorts. Forget about finding the right conditions to foster growth and happiness, because you need to stick to rigid therapy schedules, which often exceed twenty hours a week in addition to school. Forget about giving your child the space and environment to play and pursue her interests, because you need to guard against obsessions and social isolation by forcing your child to engage non-preferred activities and non-preferred people. Forget about how beautiful it is when your child flaps her hands in joy, because you need to make those hands quiet and table-ready. Forget about academics because your child needs to learn to touch her nose for a gummy bear. Forget about teaching your daughter that she can say "No!" when something doesn't feel good, because above all else, Autistic children need to learn to be compliant one-hundred percent of the time.

As a parent, I couldn't quite articulate why these directives felt wrong. I tried to express to the autism specialist that demanding constant compliance from Evelyn was not effective and that the evidence was clearly exhibited in her school "behavior," which stood in stark contrast to the happy child we knew at home. I was told that I had fewer expectations of Evelyn at home and that we were overly permissive. Then I stumbled upon a piece of writing that changed my life, and more importantly, Evelyn's life. "No You Don't" is an essay written by Maxfield Sparrow on their blog, *Unstrange Mind*,[1] and is now the basis for their book of the same title. This piece resonated so loudly with me that I wrote a piece on my own blog titled "The Cost of Compliance is Unreasonable."[2]

After writing this piece, a group of adult Autistic bloggers swooped in and saved me from the experts. Saved my daughter. They embraced my family so lovingly and kindly with their guidance based on their lived experience. They have become the best friends I have ever had. As I hungrily devoured their writing and eagerly engaged in conversation with them, my disconnected thoughts about my uneasiness with the way my daughter was being "taught" took shape. I was able to demand changes at Evelyn's school, which eventually resulted in her being infinitely more available for learning as opposed to being in a near constant state of meltdown. I was able to examine my own weaknesses as a parent to an Autistic child and make changes that had profound and far reaching effects on the quality of life for every member of our family.

It is true that every Autistic person is unique. Evelyn doesn't speak and needs twenty-four-hour-a-day support. I've received valuable guidance from adult Autistic people who have needs similar to Evelyn's. I've received valuable guidance from adults who had similar needs as children but have different needs as adults. I've received valuable guidance from adults who don't and have never appeared to be very similar to Evelyn. One of the best things about tapping into the resources that Autistic adults provide is that, unlike the experts, they don't insist that there is one way to learn and progress. They don't insist that rigid inflexible regimens be followed until a child is broken. Instead they seem to, almost universally, support the value of respecting individual needs. This results in a plethora of possible solutions, supports, accommodations, and coping mechanisms—in short, options for parenting a happy child.

I often think about how different the lives of Autistic people and their families would be if they were introduced to the wealth of information available from Autistic adults. I was thrilled to learn of this book and the doors it would potentially open, the fear it could alleviate, and the happiness that it could inspire. I hope you've read every word with an open mind and with all the love in your heart for your Autistic child. They need you to embrace all of the wonderful possibilities of their selfhood. They need your unconditional love, support, and advocacy to become their very best Autistic self.

MORÉNIKE GIWA ONAIWU, PhD(c), is a global advocate, educator, and disabled woman of color in a neurodiverse, serodifferent family. Diagnosed as Autistic in adulthood, they are a prolific writer, public speaker, and social scientist whose work focuses on meaningful community involvement, human rights, HIV research, justice, and inclusion. Morénike, a Black (Yoruba and Caboverdiano American) Xennial and mother of six, is a member of several disability executive and advisory boards who can often be found curled up reading a book, watching *Dragon Ball Z/Super* with husband Lucky, singing off-key to music, or scripting *Steven Universe* while daydreaming about being on the beach. Follow them at MorenikeGO.com and @MorenikeGO.

EMILY PAIGE BALLOU is an autistic queer woman who was diagnosed in her late twenties. A graduate of the University of Georgia, with degrees in biology and drama, and a Midwesterner at heart, she currently lives in New York City, where she works as an Off-Broadway stage manager of new plays and new musicals. Follow her on Twitter: @EPBallou.

SHARON DAVANPORT is founder and executive director of the Autistic Women & Nonbinary Network (AWN). Sharon's work encompasses several aspects of the wider disability justice movement. They have spoken before the United Nations and the White House and have received recognition from the Autistic Self Advocacy Network for their contribution to the self-advocacy movement, and the Autism Society of America for outstanding literary work of the year. Outside of Sharon's work in autistic advocacy, they have nearly a decade of experience as a social worker, and they are a parent of four diversely neurodivergent adults. Sharon is a nonbinary femme from Generation "Jones" who was born in Texas and now lives in the Midwest.

CONTRIBUTORS

B. MARTIN ALLEN Programmed to be a mid-twentieth century housewife with a second wave feminist veneer, B. Martin Allen, CFO and development editor for Autonomous Press, gleefully disappoints. Since the 1980s, in venues ranging from indie weeklies to the *Huffington Post*, Allen has been writing highly personal stories of disability's intersection with poverty, feminism, queer culture, and abuse. Keyword searches to find Martin include autistic, chronic illness, intersex, parenting, transgender, and queer.

KASSIANE ASASUMASU, a biracial Asian Xennial, diagnosed in 1986, has been doing Autistic activism since around 1999 and blogs at *Radical Neurodivergence Speaking* and *We Are Like Your Child*. Kassiane, who seeks to drag the neuroscience community kicking and screaming into the neurodiversity paradigm, lives in the Pacific Northwest and has seizure-detecting cats who are named after things found in the brain.

AMELIA "MEL" EVELYN VOICY BAGGS, known more widely by hir nickname Mel, was an influential non-speaking autistic writer, artist, and activist. Born in the California redwoods, Mel, a self-described "Hufflepuff" and "proud member of the developmental disability self-advocacy movement," who identified as queer and genderless, lived in Vermont with hir kitten until hir death in April 2020 of respiratory failure at the age of thirty-nine. As an individual with high support needs due to various medical conditions, sie believed in the value of all people, and their influential work helped to advance neurodiversity and disability rights. Mel loved painting, writing poetry and prose, crocheting, family, and friends. Mel describes some of hir early activism in an Open Source chapter, "Losing," one of their numerous published/cited works: https://www.researchgate.net/publication/337112669_Losing.

LYDIA X. Z. BROWN is an advocate, writer, community organizer, cultural worker, and lawyer whose work has focused on interpersonal and state violence against multiply marginalized disabled people living at the intersections of race, class, gender, sexuality, nation, and language. They are currently policy counsel for privacy and data at the Center for Democracy and Technology; adjunct lecturer in disability studies at Georgetown University; director of policy, advocacy, and external affairs at the Autistic Women & Nonbinary Network; and founder and volunteer director of the Fund for Community Reparations for Autistic People of Color's Interdependence, Survival, and Empowerment. They were co-editor of *All the Weight of Our Dreams: On Living Racialized Autism*. Their writing appears in numerous community and scholarly publications, including *Monstering Magazine*, *gal-dem*, *Asian American Literary Review*, and *Disability Studies Quarterly*. Their next independent project is Disability Justice Wisdom Tarot.

MALLORY, or **MAL, CRUZ** is a mixed, autistic individual from southern New York. She runs the autism blog, *Things That Cause Autism*. She appeared in an episode of Dylan Marron's *Shutting Down Bullsh*t* about autism. In 2018, she spoke at the United Nations for World Autism Awareness Day. She recently moved to Japan.

ALEXANDRA FORSHAW is a bisexual British autistic mother of an adult autistic daughter, an artist, designer, musician, writer, and software developer. An avid volunteer, she sits on the boards of the neurodivergent-led charity Flow Observatorium and the nonprofit Autistic Inclusive Meets. She is a trans woman who lives in Hampshire, UK. Follow her on Twitter: @myautisticdance; Instagram: alex.m.forshaw; and https://myautisticdance.blog.

KAREN LEAN is a software professional and artist living in Boston, Massachusetts. She contributes to the Asperger/Autism Network as a volunteer and as a professional speaker. She has also served on its board of directors. Her talks have included a keynote on the role of a supportive environment in relationships, and on meaningful employment. Karen is originally from Toronto, Canada.

KATIE LEVIN is a straight, white, autistic Generation Xer who serves as the social media manager for Aspiritech (https://www.aspiritech.org), a not-for-profit organization that employs adults on the autism spectrum to perform software, QA testing, and similar IT industry tasks. Having lost both parents by early adulthood, Katie, who was diagnosed with Asperger's in her twenties, created one of the first groups for autistic adults in the Chicago area while obtaining her bachelor's degree in liberal arts (studio arts minor) from Northeastern Illinois University.

DUSYA L. is a straight, white millennial with an Asperger's diagnosis from the northeastern region of the US. Having personally struggled with the early death of both parents as well as academic and work challenges, Dusya is passionate about resources such as mental health services, family support, and career coaching. She is active in advocacy, works in healthcare, and attends college part time.

HALEY MOSS is an autistic attorney and the author of *Middle School: The Stuff Nobody Tells You About* and *A Freshman Survival Guide for College Students with Autism Spectrum Disorders: The Stuff Nobody Tells You About.* A millennial who lives in South Florida, Haley spends an awful lot of time thinking about neurodiversity at work and making law practice more inclusive for people with disabilities. Follow her at http://haleymoss.net; @haleymossart (FB, Twitter, IG).

BRIGID RANKOWSKI (mixed pronouns) is a queer artist, educator, and advocate living in Maine. She obtained a master's degree from Nova Southeastern University after her undergraduate studies at

Cornell College in Iowa. Their master's degree is in developmental disabilities, with an emphasis on leadership and advocacy. Brigid participates on state and national disability boards. She is the founder of The Way We Move, a social circus promoting the circus arts for marginalized communities. When not doing advocacy work, Brigid is an experienced circus performer.

ONDREA MARISA ROBINSON is an African American millennial who was diagnosed with pervasive developmental disorder-not otherwise specified at three years old. An autistic advocate, seasoned writer, and speaker who identifies as a straight woman, Ondrea loves Eeyore from *Winnie the Pooh* (even though she's not gloomy like Eeyore—she's happy!) and also loves the color pink.

KAYLA RODRIGUEZ is a lesbian Puerto Rican millennial self-advocate. A BDI (Bobby Dodd Institute) Ambassador, a former LEND trainee, and a recipient of the Golden Goal Goldie Award for Best Young Community Advocate, she is also involved with ASAA (Autism Self-Advocacy of Atlanta, an affiliate group of ASAN), AWN, and leads the PCORI/Emory Women's autism group. Kayla won the Bobby Dodd Institute Empowers Luminaries Award in 2020. Twitter: @theKwomanrules; Instagram: @kaylarod; LinkedIn: https://www.linkedin.com/in/kayla-rodriguez-139b0b169.

VICTORIA M. RODRÍGUEZ-ROLDÁN, JD, is a millennial in the DC region whose work focuses on the intersections of issues affecting transgender people with disabilities and mental illness, anti-trans workplace discrimination, and gun violence prevention from a social justice lens. She is a Latina (Puerto Rican) bisexual transwoman who has been in trans advocacy the entirety of her adult life, including advocacy in Puerto Rico and in Maine. Twitter: @yovimi.

BETH RYAN is a straight, white Generation Xer who lives in New England. Beth is a mom to Evelyn, an autistic teen girl, and her younger sister Maxine. She blogs at LoveExplosions.net.

JENNIFER ST. JUDE is a consultant, a university/professional conference lecturer, an author, and an advocate. She holds a bachelor's of social work degree and teaching credentials. Jennifer presents workshops on adult autism topics that focus on improving treatment and strategies. She, along with an occupational therapist, created a model called CTESS to improve treatment outcomes for professionals and clients with developmental disabilities. Jennifer was raised in Brooklyn, New York, and now lives in Lancaster, California. Her personal journey with autism and parenting children on the spectrum offers a unique perspective into this uncharted topic of autism and women and girls. Jennifer is the creator of the Facebook page Autism Grows Up. Follow her at https://www.facebook.com/AutismGrowsUpHere or at her website: www.JenniferStJude.com.

AMYTHEST SCHABER, or **MYTH**, is an autistic writer, artist, and public speaker. They became known in the autism community as an explainer-of-things through their blog, Neurowonderful, and as a bridge between autistic folk and the non-autistic people who love them with their YouTube video series, *Ask an Autistic*. These days they play a lot of *D&D*, read many books, and write loads of words. They live in the Greater Vancouver area with their best friend and partner, Marvin, and their big black cat, Jiji. Link: www.youtube.com/user/neurowonderful.

AMY SEQUENZIA is a non-speaking Autistic, multiply disabled activist, writer, international presenter, and executive board member of the Autistic Self Advocacy Network. Amy's authorship includes *Communication Alternatives in Autism: Perspectives on Typing and Spelling Approaches for the Nonspeaking*, *Typed Words, Loud Voices* (which Amy also co-edited), essays, and poetry on civil and human rights that has been featured in books and as guest contributions to media outlets and blogs, including *HuffPost*, *Catalyst Journal*, *Stanford Daily*, *AWN Network*, *Ollibean*, *Pacific Standard Magazine*, and a personal blog (nonspeakingautisticspeaking.blogspot.com).

KAYLA SMITH is a Black, autistic, Generation Z self-advocate who has been actively involved in disability activism since 2017. She promotes neurodiversity and highlights autistic people of color at local colleges, online, and in the media. Kayla, who lives in North Carolina, created #AutisticBlackPride to celebrate and embrace Black and autistic pride at the same time. Twitter: @BeingKayla Smith; Facebook: Kayla Smith; Instagram: @beingmskayla; Tik-Tok: @autistickayla; YouTube: Autistic Kayla: The Opinion of a Black Autistic Woman.

LYNNE SORAYA writes about her experiences as an autistic adult and the issues facing women on the autism spectrum. She is the author of the book *Living Independently on the Autism Spectrum* and the "Asperger's Diary" blog in *Psychology Today*, and lives in the Pacific Southwest. Follow her @lynnesoraya.

MAXFIELD SPARROW is the author of two books about the Autistic lived experience and editor of the anthology *Spectrums: Autistic Transgender People in Their Own Words*. Sparrow, a white Generation Xer who identifies as metagender and demipansexual, holds an MFA in creative writing and poetics from Naropa University and continues their education in Colorado, with the goal of becoming a Certified Poetry Therapist. Follow their work at maxfieldsparrow.com and unstrangemind.com.

JANE STRAUSS, a woman of Middle Eastern origin living in Minnesota for over forty years, lived her life on the spectrum without Portfolio (aka diagnosis) until the age of fifty-two. In the interim, she gained several college and professional degrees and worked in nonprofits, advocacy, law, education, and as a stay-at-home mom to five kids (all likely on the spectrum), and as a home educator. She has been in two long-term intimate relationships and spends her time as a photographer, writer, and home educator, with forays into research, professional presentations, and legal practice. She recently began using her Autistic superpowers of pattern identification, persistence, problem solving, and scripting to work as a Census Bureau field representative.

HEIDI WANGELIN (HW) is a white millennial disability rights advocate and an activist in Silver Spring, Maryland, who used to live in Seattle. Heidi is a RespectAbility and AmeriCorps member alumna, where she worked on disability policy and outreach. She has a bachelor's degree in culture, literature, and arts and in Disability Studies, and she has been published in a poetry anthology. When Heidi is not working or spending time with friends, she enjoys reading and music.

LEI WILEY-MYDSKE is an autistic and otherwise disabled mom, wife, neurodiversity librarian, the Community Outreach Coordinator at AWN Network, activist, artist, and gendervague writer from the Pacific Northwest. Follow Lei's work at Neurodiversitylibrary.org.

JEAN WINEGARDNER is an autistic woman who lives with her husband, three neurodivergent children, and a largish number of cats near DC. She writes about autism, running, and small, amusing rodents on her blog (Stimeyland.com). Jean's MA in print journalism from the University of Southern California and love of filling out forms often comes in handy at her day job (office manager for the Autistic Self Advocacy Network). She enjoys reading and movies (especially if they're apocalyptic and zombie-based) and detests long walks on the beach, because, ick, sand.

ACKNOWLEDGMENTS

We would like to express our immense gratitude to every single individual who has been involved with envisioning, developing, finalizing, promoting, and republishing our anthology. Your support has meant the world to us.

We especially wish to thank Corina Becker, Mara Fritts, and Lori Berkowitz, AWN's Working Board Members, who have held our hands and cheered us on throughout this entire process; Erin Casey for all of your creativity and innovation; Karen Muriuki for your tireless activism not only in Kenya, but across the globe ... your efforts provide continuous encouragement to all of us at AWN; and Court Alison Falk for your authenticity and for providing an invaluable perspective that helps inform AWN's work.

We're also sending a huge thank-you and love to our family, friends, and all the important people in our lives for your endless patience and positivity throughout this journey. You put up with our never-ending virtual meetings, email discussions, lengthy phone calls, and late-night editing sessions, and for that we are grateful!

Many thanks to the team at Beacon Press for believing in us, especially Joanna Green, Alison Rodriguez, Melissa Nasson, and Marcy Barnes. We also wish to acknowledge our cherished friend and colleague Lydia X. Z. Brown for their involvement in our initial communications with Beacon.

To the many people who helped make our first anthology a reality, thank you from all of us at AWN for believing in the importance of this timeless and much-needed resource. A special shout-out goes out to Haley Moss for creating our original cover art and to our friends Jess Wilson and Beth Ryan for sharing their perspectives as parents of autistic children in the foreword and conclusion.

Last but not least, this book would not be possible without the amazing authors of this anthology itself, whose open-heartedness and honesty filled these chapters with vibrant and heartfelt vulnerability.

NOTES

FOREWORD

1. Jess Wilson, "The Gift of Perspective," A Diary of a Mom, March 31, 2008, https://adiaryofamom.com/2008/03/31/the-gift-of-perception/.

2. Anonymous, "Asperger's: My Life as an Earthbound Alien," CNN .com, March 28, 2008, http://www.cnn.com/2008/HEALTH/conditions/03 /28/autism.essay/index.html.

CHAPTER 3 What Autistic Girls Wish Their Parents Knew About Friendship

1. Elizabeth Crary, *My Name Is Not Dummy* (Seattle: Parenting Press, 1983), http://www.parentingpress.com/b_cps.html.

CHAPTER 4 What Your Daughter Deserves

1. "Allistic" is a neologism for "non-autistic."

CHAPTER 10 A Particular Way of Being

1. Asperger/Autism Network, http://www.aane.org, accessed August 29, 2020.

CHAPTER 11 A Daughter's Journey: Lessons, Honesty, and Love

1. Autism Discussion Page, Facebook, https://www.facebook.com/autism discussionpage/timeline, accessed August 29, 2020.

CHAPTER 17 Ten Things I Wish My Parents Had Known When I Was Growing Up

1. Lorna Wing and Amitta Shah, "Catatonia in Autistic Spectrum Disorders," *British Journal of Psychiatry* 176, no. 4 (April 2000): 357–62, https://doi .org/10.1192/bjp.176.4.357.

2. Center on Human Policy, *The Community Imperative: A Refutation of All Arguments In Support of Institutionalizing Anybody Because of Mental Retardation* (Syracuse, NY: Syracuse University, 1979), http://mn.gov/mnddc /parallels2/pdf/70s/79/79-ctr-human-policy-comm-imp.pdf.

3. ADAPT, https://adapt.org/, accessed October 5, 2020.

CHAPTER 19 The View from Outside the Window

1. Autistic Self Advocacy Network, http://www.autisticadvocacy.org, accessed August 29, 2020.

CHAPTER 22 **Keep Her Safe; Let Her Fly Free**

1. Teka J. Harris, "Behavioral Momentum," May Institute, https://www.may institute.org/news/acl/asd-and-dd-child-focused/behavioral-momentum, accessed August 11, 2020.

2. Ariane Zurcher, "Emma Refuses to Get Off the Bus and a Self Advocate Is Born," *Emma's Hope Book*, blog, September 11, 2012, http://emmashopebook.com/2012/09/11/emma-refuses-to-get-off-the-bus-and-a-self-advocate-is-born.

CHAPTER 27 **A Parents' Guide to Being Transgender and Autistic**

1. Lynn Conway, "How Frequently Does Transsexualism Occur?" original article posted January 30, 2001, http://ai.eecs.umich.edu/people/conway/TS/TSprevalence.html.

2. J. Strang et al., "Increased Gender Variance in Autism Spectrum Disorders and Attention Deficit Hyperactivity Disorder," *Archives of Sexual Behavior* 43, no. 8 (March 2014): 1525–33, https://doi.org/10.1007/s10508-014-0285-3.

Conclusion

1. Maxfield Sparrow, "No You Don't," *Unstrange Mind*, January 27, 2013, https://unstrangemind.wordpress.com/2013/01/27/no-you-dont.

2. Beth Ryan, "The Cost of Compliance Is Unreasonable," *love explosions*, January 30, 2013, http://loveexplosions.net/2013/01/30/the-cost-of-compliance-is-unreasonable.